WOMEN LIKE ME

A Tribute to the Brave and Wise

JULIE FAIRHURST

ROCK STAR PUBLISHING

www.womenlikemestories.com

Contents

"For over a decade she stood there once a while, gazing at the infinite sea, on-call to engulf whoever jumps.

And then, a day, she dived into it, with fragmented emotions, and worn-out soul, to a novel desire, to an unseasoned growth, enroute of a superior essence."

Irfa Rahat

Introduction

JULIE FAIRHURST

"The greatest tragedy of a person's life is dying without ever knowing who he or she really is." - Myles Munroe

This is a great thought-provoking quote and very fitting for this volume of Women Like Me – A tribute to the brave and wise.

Do you know yourself? Really know who you are? Most women I ask do not. They may know their height and weight and eye color. This is usually what they describe when asked. Or they may give a title, a wife, a mother, a grandmother, a daughter, or a friend. But this is not who they really are. These are labels or descriptions used to describe ourselves.

You may have read this, and now your thinking about yourself. You may not know who you are, and that's okay. You not alone. Many people out there are not sure of who they are. When a person experiences trauma of some kind, it can shut down inner growth and cause you to freeze. And, if you are living your life in survival mode, you may not be aware of it as you may not have had the time to stop, relax and take time to work on yourself. You may have been so consumed in taking care of others and your daily responsibilities that you never got a chance to get to know who you are.

This would describe most of our lives. In this crazy but beautiful world we live in, and there is seldom time for self-reflection. That is not until the kids move out, a death, a divorce, illness, or even retirement from a long career finds us alone, with time on our hands. We may then start to look inward at who we really are and what we want out of the rest of our lives.

The women who have written in his volume of Women Like Me are women who know who they are! Their lives took them on a journey that forced them to look inside themselves and discover who they were as a woman. How to fight to get what they wanted and needed. And what they want for their future.

We all only have two choices. Stay stuck or wake up and get living! These resilient women all decided to get on with their lives to better themselves and their loved ones.

So many of us, women, and men want to be a better, more improved version of our current selves. Is it any wonder that the self-improvement industry has grown into a massive $10 billion industry? You see, the one person who you will spend the rest of your life with is you. And hopefully, you can love and like who you are because you can't get away from yourself. Our friends, family members, co-workers, they all come and go, but you will have to deal with your thoughts and actions until the day you die.

This book is a tribute to the brave and wise women who dared to share their stories with us. These women have come to know who they are and what they want or need in their lives. They have found their voices to speak up for themselves, to speak up for their loved ones, and to take care of themselves. This is a lesson that many never learn, and that is truly sad.

If you are not striving to constantly better yourself, you may become unhappy with your life because you are not happy with yourself. And if this happens, you may become angry, bitter, and not a nice person to be around. You may chase away those you are closest to you.

Facing your shortcomings, your past mistakes, or your past trauma leads to healing your soul. When you deal with the skeletons in your closet, peace will come to you. I have realized in life that it takes precious energy to hide, for whatever is or has happened to you. When you face life and choose to be responsible for your happiness and give up caring what others think, this is when you shift your energy use into high gear. Now your energy can be used to advance you in your life rather than hold you back.

We can not rely on other people to make us happy. We can only make ourselves happy. Part of dealing with your life and refusing to be shut down is what will truly make you happy. Taking responsibility for how we deal with what life throws at us is empowering.

The women in Women Like Me have all learned valuable life lessons from their experiences and risen with immense courage to tell their stories, hoping that they can help another. When we write our stories, we can heal and release ourselves from our past. And, knowing that there may be a woman out there reading her story, she hopes it can help encourage self-growth and awareness. It is an important reason for the women in Women Like Me to tell their stories. Each woman desires to help another woman in her life journey.

The writers in Women Like Me are like all women in one way or another. They are women who have loved and have lost, only to love again. They are women who experienced devastating illnesses and find peace. They are women who have dealt with the ultimate betrayal but heal themselves and not allow it to wreck their lives. They are just women, women like me and women like you.

"You have to keep breaking your heart until it opens." Rumi

The stories you are about to read are true-life stories of a chapter in each woman's life. These are stories the writers felt they needed to write about to release themselves from any issues in their past that may have been holding them back from living their best lives.

They also chose stories that would help another woman who may be experiencing a similar situation. The writers in Women Like Me all have a strong desire to help others on their journey in life.

Some of the stories are of awakenings, finding themselves, realizing their worth, and learning to love themselves for who they are today despite where they have come from or what they have dealt with.

At times, readers can be triggered by a word, statement, story, or event. An emotional trigger can be a person, situation, or experience, but the emotion rendered to process it is intense and exaggerated. The stories are emotional and moving and can bring up feelings you may not have felt in years or possibly never felt.

If this happens to you, you may want to reach out and talk to someone about how you are feeling or what may have triggered your emotional reaction.

You can reach out to your local crisis line, doctor, friend, teacher, counselor, parent, spouse, and even adult children. There is always someone out there who is willing to listen and who wants to help. Take care of yourself.

If you want to find out more about the book series Women Like Me, make a book purchase, the authors, their stories, and how you can write your story, please check out the Women Like Me website.

www.womenlikemestories.com

22 Vials
FROM 60 TO ZERO ENERGY AWARENESS

"How truly magical is the human spirit that can take you through the fight of your life and have you feeling humbled and grateful and excited all at the same time."
Christine Hayden

"**I**" was BUSY. Working as a full-time Realtor alongside my husband, the hours were crazy, but the job was exciting. We were empty nesters now, so it was perfect! We just had to keep ourselves watered and fed. We thrived off the fast pace, the interactions with clients, meeting new people, comradery with our colleagues. Life was great!

No one really expects to be "fine" one minute and on death's doorstep the next. It's a feeling that is inexplicable, unbelievable, and surreal. I felt like I was floating outside my body. We are all human, and although we think it will never happen to us. It can. I was probably the least likely candidate to get a serious illness. I've been annoying my family and friends for years with my perfect eating, organics, exercise, and using natural products, all the while harping on everyone that I loved to do the same.

I suppose there were signs. I was tired, but we were working crazy hours. I was having a hard time remembering things, but I'm not a spring chicken anymore. The physical signs were on my legs, red spots, and bruises on my knees. The past couple of days, I noticed unusual bleeding in my mouth and other oddities; so, I knew I needed to get checked and probably shouldn't put this one-off. I quipped to a friend after searching Google. "I either have a heat rash or leukemia" Off I went to the clinic just in case, and so it started; a series of events that put me on what I believe is MY journey and the trajectory that saved me from my life.

I visited a new clinic in the neighborhood and got right in. I had never met the doctor before, and he didn't seem to have the people skills to say hello or ask me my name. I sat down and awkwardly adjusted my clothing so he could have a look at my legs. "They look weird," he said and asked me if I had shaved them recently. "Ummmm. I don't think that's the problem here?" "Dr. Google said I should probably get a blood test," I suggested. My underwhelmed doctor wrote me a script, and off I went to a small local lab nearby.

When I arrived at the lab, it wasn't busy, but the power went out as I was signing in. "I don't have time for this." I sat there thinking. "Do I stay, or do I go now?" There's another lab across town; it's 20 minutes away and usually packed with people. "Patience is a virtue," my mother always said, and the best case is to wait it out here. The friendly lady sitting next to me agrees, and she stays with me. We waited an hour for the power to come back on, they took my blood, and I was out of there. I had a listing appointment and some prep work to finish up for a 6 pm appointment that evening, so back to work I went.

Arriving home after my appointment, it was 7:15 pm, and my phone rang as I walked in the front door. It was a doctor on the line. "Kimberley Mallory?" We've reviewed your lab results, and you need to go straight to emergency!" WTF?? Okay! "Can you please let my family doctor know what's going on?" My mind was racing… this is probably NOT GOOD. My husband and I ran around the house gathering a bag, and we raced down to our local hospital.

They saw me coming a mile away, promptly handed me a mask, and whisked me away into isolation. Two nurses sat me in a chair, rolled up a cart, and drained me of whatever blood I had. Twenty-two vials, to be exact.

I had been in isolation in the emergency ward for two nights getting blood transfusions and tests when my family doctor arrived. I was relieved to see her, but I watched as she was looking over her shoulder at me with grave concern. She was on the phone and kept glancing back at me and gesturing toward the computer. They were trying to get some sort of a bone marrow test booked, and nothing was available. It would have to wait until Monday. The look on my doctor's face told me that I wouldn't make it to any appointments on Monday. I didn't have that much time. I was given a form to fill out. At the end of the form, it asked if I had any special requests. I wrote down: "Please don't let me die!!!" I thought it was funny. My husband did not, but I've always used humor in any bad situation to lighten the mood.

My Doctor, My Saviour

Within 12 hours, my family doctor had pulled some strings and had me in an ambulance to Vancouver General Hospital. I had been midway through a blood transfusion, and they needed a nurse to accompany me for the ride. It was a battle of wills since my nurse was getting off shift, and no one wanted to make the round trip to Vancouver. The nurses were yelling and arguing with each other about who would be the one to go. It was quite entertaining. In the end, the poor nurse who was probably just finishing up a twelve-hour shift lost the battle. There was no time to wait, and they started rolling me out. I said goodbye and joked that I'm sure they got me out of there quickly because I was the pain in the ass that kept pulling the emergency bell that gets ten people in your room at once. In the ambulance, I quipped with the nurse who was tending to me and gave her advice on dealing with depressed teenagers.

I ended up in Vancouver General Hospital on the 15th floor at the Bone Marrow Transplant/Leukemia ward. I arrived knowing that my Bone Marrow had "given up." My

T-cells were attacking my good blood cells. They thought I had Leukemia or Aplastic Anemia. Coincidentally, my cat, whom I adore, got sick last year, and they thought she had Leukemia too. It turned out to be Anemia, and she recovered nicely, so obviously, I was hoping it would be the latter of the two diseases, and we could have that extra bonding experience. Plus, with her recovery, she got a daily dose of fish to keep her iron up, so her life is better for what she had to go through. If my cat can beat this and come out better for it, so can I.

I arrived in Acute Care, and the tests began. My life as I knew it had just ended. Now I'm a "doer," and I'm told that even after I get out of the hospital, I can't drive, I can't do laundry, I can't cook, I can't garden, I can't be around animals, I can't be around people, cats, babies. My immune system is gone. I'm going to be in the hospital for a while. They are pumping me full of antibiotics, and my blood counts have tanked to dangerously low levels. I need regular transfusions of red blood and platelets. Great.

I am in a studio apartment, by myself, on the 15th floor of the hospital overlooking the city. Not so bad. This pad would cost at least $2000 a month with this city view. The doctor arrives, and we discuss my situation and a treatment plan. It's going to be a long haul, and I can't pretend this isn't happening, much as I like to sweep things under the rug and downplay everything. I'm down for the count, and I can't hide it or fake it this time. I have to deal with the reality of it and what that means for myself, my clients, my family, and my friends.

Everything was a blur, and by this time, my family was in chaos, freaking out because "I'm gonna die." I told the doctors, "Do whatever you need to do; I won't complain." I was trying to be positive, but outside the hospital walls, my family and friends were falling apart and losing it. Being sensitive to "bad" energy, I thought, "They are either going to give themselves a heart attack, or they are going to curse me with their negativity, and I'm doomed." My spidey senses told me that I had to tame the beast, I'm not dead yet, and I'm not taking any chances. Positive thoughts ONLY. I'm taking it one day at a time. I'm in good hands, and all I can do is 'be.' They tell me I've got a 70% chance. I plan on taking that 30% to work the energy, stay positive, and round it up to 100%. I am going to beat this.

One by one, I called each of my family members and told them that they need to switch their thought process from negative to positive. Their worry, strife, and panic are going to kill them surely before it's my time to go, and this isn't about them. This is about me. It's my battle to fight, and I need them to remain calm so I can be calm. I need their positive energy to get through this. I also had to come out to my clients and friends. Like, tell the world I'm down for the count because that is my reality. I don't want a bunch of people crying or offering sympathy. I need to focus on my new task at hand, which is to get better, so I officially declared myself Princess Kim. I made the announcement to my Facebook world then promptly put my phone on DO NOT DISTURB.

" So I'm in VGH for the long haul. I have Aplastic Anemia, and I start treatment tomorrow. I will need to stay close to the hospital,

which means I finally get that apartment near the city I've always wished for. I'm going to be taking six months off to get better, and I officially declare myself a Princess, and I will do nothing but allow people to take care of me, so you may now refer to me as Princess Kim. My phone is muted, but I do read the messages and respond on Princess time. *I'm taking all positive thoughts and prayers * I cannot take visitors as my immune system is down. * If you want to help, please donate blood and get on the list to become a stem cell/ bone marrow donor. *Feel good comments only. I am not looking for sympathy. Just love and support....

And so, my journey began. With a 70% Chance of survival and knowing without a doubt that 30% of this was on me, I wasn't going to fuck it up. Everyone I knew was praying and sending good vibes, and it felt like a good start. My son-in-law gave me an indigenous leather-wrapped healing crystal with a feather, hand-made by a chief. I had my "tools" and books for inspirational reading that freed my mind of worry and gave me hope. Every day I cried tears of gratitude for the doctors and nurses that were working to save my life. Every day I thanked God for the prayer warriors that were sending me the energy I needed to carry on.

I have always "tried" to meditate, and sometimes it worked, and sometimes it would just stress me out that I couldn't calm my mind enough to focus on it. It came to me that I should ask my friends and family to send me their good energy between 7 pm and 8 pm one evening. I was going to harness those good vibes and meditate on getting better. Of all the mystical and meditative experiences I have had in my life, that was the most profound. I reached a level of transcendence that I had never felt before. It was as though my body had lifted off the bed and was floating in white light. I could feel the intense energy flowing through me. It was bright, and my tears flowed like a cleansing of all the bad while a renewal was taking place. This went on for a full hour. I had the sense that this was meant to be my journey—something I'm supposed to experience for me to get to a better place. The divine timing of everything thus far had given me the clues I needed to know that this was happening for a reason, and I accepted that.

Now that's not to say that being sick doesn't come with some negative emotions. It naturally comes with a feeling of immense guilt and grief. The pain and worry inflicted on my family were much worse for me than my experience of dealing with the illness. The guilt of not being there and everyone having to pick up the slack. Knowing that everyone was stressed out because of me is something that I cried a lot about, but I have had to learn to forgive myself. I am loved, and I love.

My journey lasted 16 months. The first round of treatment resulted in a partial recovery which wasn't enough to sustain. So it was decided that I would need a Bone Marrow Transplant. I was extremely lucky. My brother was a 10 out of 10 match and agreed to donate his marrow. I was back in the hospital for this life-saving procedure on February 20th, 2021, EXACTLY one year to the day that I was admitted to VGH for my initial treatment. Now, this is serious Twilight Zone material and reinforces my belief that this was meant to be my journey.

I was very careful not to give energy to the negative, and I used rituals and therapy to right my mind to focus on healing: meditations, healing stones, energy clearings, chakra work, reiki, counseling, hypnotherapy, inspirational stories. I do not talk about the negative until it is in the past and it can no longer hurt me. Even then, it is discussed as a lesson and not a complaint. I have been a work in progress, and I am thankful for the changes this has brought me. Over time, I realized I was turning into the person I WANTED to be. There was no more battle of Ego vs Soul anymore. I was stripped free of ego, and my heart was overflowing with love, acceptance, gratitude, and a calmness I had never felt before. I was able to release the stress, worry, and fear. I am a different person today, and I'm thankful for this experience which has left me in awe of the medical system, the doctors and nurses, and the power that we have inside of us to help create our positive outcome.

Before my transplant, a friend asked me, aren't you afraid? My answer: "There is no fear if you don't fear death." I can't predict the future, so why fear death? No one truly knows when their time is up. Once I was able to let go of the fear, I felt like a kid in a candy store. As I excitedly wrote to a friend: "I feel like Scrooge waking up on Christmas Morning." Do I want to go back to my old life? Not really. I'm in a renewal phase, and I'm wide open. For the first time in my entire life, I am at peace which I believe translates to having reached a level of consciousness that could best be described as enlightenment.

We are all here for an undefined amount of time and to learn to live a peaceful existence is mindfulness. To have an appreciation for the little things should be a goal everyone should strive for. This experience has changed me. I am the light; I am centered, self-aware, pure consciousness, free. I am my higher self. I am liberated. I'm in a high state of energy. Open, grateful, enjoying the depth of experience, I'm balanced. Intuitive, spiritual, reborn, whole. This is the "me" that I've always wanted to be, and it doesn't get much better than that.

Adversity truly is growth.

Kim Mallory

This Crazy Little Thing Called ADHD.

HOW A LATE DIAGNOSIS CHANGED A NURSE ENTREPRENEURS LIFE

"The truth is something that burns. It burns off dead wood. And people don't like having the dead wood brunt off, often because they're 95 percent dead wood. When you have something to say... Silence is a lie."
Jordan Peterson

Okay, So here goes nothing...

Let me tell you a little story about a girl who had what you may call a bit of a whirlwind, tornado-like kind of life. About a girl, who was parented by a wonderful mother, and a hard-working father. I was quite bright, very imaginative, musical, talkative, bold, and kind. I had just as good of a chance as any; at least, this is what most people in my life told me. Yet there was this thing. This unknown thing that I never knew was an actual thing. That kept my life in this constant whirlwind that I eventually just considered "my normal." And this "thing" that no one really knew what it was, or even knew it had a name—created by what I call a very exciting thing. So challenging at times yet fulfilling in the same sentence, and I wouldn't change it one bit!

So this little thing that I didn't know was a thing is called ADHD. Also known as Attention Deficit Hyperactive Disorder. And, I miss Vannessa Fowler, RN, businesswoman, and mother of two... I now know I 100% have this disorder!

And WOWEE! Was that a mind-bender moment when I got diagnosed with this at the ripe age of 39! Thirty-nine? How in the heck did I make it to 39 years old and never had this missing puzzle piece ever offered to me? Although, of course, I have ADHD, wasn't it obvious?

Not so much? Don't I own a business? And, am I not an Emergency Room nurse? Aren't I also a shoe expert? Can size anyone for a good sports bra while caring for two girls' and a household while having on and off relationships. And, on and off, GREAT amazing ideas! Some failed, yet some did so well. Hence the carefree life I have been able to live unapologetically. Yet, with so many apologies along the way.

It was a moment of sadness, relief, excitement, and enlightening all at the same time. There was even a slight feeling of resentment momentarily, that no one in my life. None of those teachers, doctors, or counselors ever told me I had it! How could they not have noticed? Why wasn't I told if they knew? The thing is, they didn't know. I can imagine these are all "normal" feelings anyone would feel if they were diagnosed with something late in the game that made their puzzle complete.

All those struggles I had growing up that never entirely made any sense to me at the time made sense to me now. Today, after learning so much more about this ADHD, I hold no anger or resentment to anyone in my life that didn't know. I have forgiven myself for my idiosyncrasies and my compulsiveness/impulsiveness. I have learned to love this about myself. It made me become the woman I love today. I learned so much more about ADHD that I never knew and honestly know it will be a forever learning process.

I look back at my whole life, and I laugh out loud sometimes because it's now so blatantly obvious I have ADHD. I feel even more empathy for what my poor mother went through with me, hahaha, especially during my rebellious teenage years. I was a force to be reckoned with and an Aries to boot. Again my poor mother. I got my karma handed back to me when I was blessed with a daughter who was just like me (story to follow). Maybe I should tell you now? My daughter was diagnosed just a year before I was. Did you know, a person with ADHD is up to 50% likely to have a child with the same problem? I must have been in denial because even after my daughter's diagnosis, I seemed not to recognize immediately I had the same issues.

Okay, back to the story. So growing up, I was very well supported. I was fortunate enough to have loving and very responsible parents. I had two brothers, and I was the oldest. Thank goodness my mother was super organized, driven, and has been an entrepreneur her whole life. Because she was such a take-charge kind of lady and structured that helped us kids along the way. I can see now how again, my ADHD would have been missed. I would guess most of you reading this were of the idea that ADHD was primarily boys. And you are correct with that statement.

You also may think of ADHD kids like that little boy in your classroom who disrupted the teacher. Who was constantly fidgeting in his seat, always in trouble; you may have even felt bad for him because he was always that kid who was always making people angry or annoyed. I will sadly admit, this was my understanding of ADHD. And I can tell you right now; I was NOT that hyperactive child. As a matter of fact, in my elementary years, I was so shy, I hardly talked in school. However, something changed during puberty because I was the polar opposite in high school.

My mother owned a commercial bakery, and I couldn't count the number of times I burned 100 loaves of bread because I was too distracted chatting on the phone or doing something way more interesting than watching bread bake. If I were to take a guess, I would say at least 100 times in my teenage years; my mother had to stay up another few hours baking new loaves of bread, so she had it the following day in her bakery. The emotions in the house during that time were a bit prickly.I remember my mother pleading with me to please just remember that this is the family's income, that I needed to remember. And yet, I had FULL intention to remember because I valued our family income. But I really would forget.

My report cards often read: She is academically strong but needs to apply herself more frequently, often LATE, constantly interrupting or talking in class, unorganized, missing assignments. I'd get an A on a test one day and fail a similar test the next day. I frustrated my mother because she didn't understand why I couldn't stay on task, follow-through, and forget things. She didn't understand why I could do so well some days and look like an incapable person the next. It was never consistent, and it never made sense to her or me. But it makes so much sense now.

I remember people saying; you're such a bright girl. Why won't you apply yourself to things all the time? Only some-times? We can see when you do something, and you can excel. Why would you not want to do that with all the things in your life? They were correct! When I became hyper-focused on anything, I would put 100% and above into it and make it happen. I could pull off some pretty impressive achievements if I'm allowed to toot my own horn.

So those days, I would feel pretty good about myself, then days would follow, and I wasn't that driven person anymore, and I would disappoint myself. And I would tend to disappoint others. I remember a point in my life that I had just accepted I am and would disappoint people more often than not. I got just used to people being annoyed or upset with me. It didn't feel good, but it became my reality. I used to tell myself. Well, I'm not everyone's cup of tea. If you like me, you like me. If we click, we click. Again I never intended to make it difficult. I wholeheartedly was doing what I could at the time. And I was lucky enough to have people who loved and liked me that I was always okay in the end.

Trust me! My nursing instructors got annoyed at times. My JUST on-time arrivals, my last-minute assignments, my sometimes daydream moments where I literally have taken something you've said to me and now have three or four new thoughts also running in my mind. It was, again, a strange feeling to realize that most adults don't have this problem. Only about 4% of adults have ADHD, and out of that 4%, less than half are women. And, if you're an ADHD'er who has more predominantly inattentive traits, it can easily be undiagnosed. Now times are changing, and these things are more screened in school.

Teenage years-The Hormonal Queen. My ADHD came out tenfold. Now, remember, though, we didn't know I had ADHD. At the time, I was considered an out-of-the-blue, impulsive, overly emotional, oppositional defiance like a girl... who was always on the go, living a carefree life. And doing what she pleased. I ran away from home more times than I can even count. I skipped classes even more than that. The parents of my friends liked and disliked me. I was sometimes the blame for distracting "their" kids into poor behavior and choices.

They likely were partly right. I was, and still am, a high energy charismatic type person when I got my eye on the prize. Whether it's to hang out with those cute boys during the afternoon or attend that MUST go to a party on Friday night, nothing could stop me. I'd put everything important on the back burner and would be hyper-focused. I was not even thinking about the consequences. Now part of the lack of foresight is simply a developmental stage of all adolescence. I do understand this. Our frontal lobes are not fully developed into early adulthood. The action/consequence and future pathways are still developing. And with a person with ADHD, it can make that process a bit more challenging.

In high school, I had a variety of types of friends. I got along with most people, but my personality was an acquired taste. I had so many detentions, and I had been expelled a couple of times. Yet, I would still pass my grades. I would plug along and still float in life. I excelled in piano. I started to play the piano when I was only four and completed my grade eight royal conservatory. I won either first or second place in all my competitions in Alberta while growing up. I was also the same person who went out of her way to record herself practicing and playing it loud enough to trick her mother into thinking she had finished her practicing so she could go hang out with friends. I think I got away with it? Haha, who really knows.

I had a tough time regulating my emotions as a teenager and still struggled with it into adulthood. I was diagnosed with depression as a young teenager and put on antidepressants immediately. I had intermittent counseling, which initially didn't help me at all. Knowing that many of the things I was struggling with put me into depression could have been worked on differently. A lot of the anxiety was also secondary to how my thought processes worked and the environment around me trying to navigate me and me trying to navigate it. But no one knew, including me.

So here are some of the struggles I had as a teenager. I remember feeling very passionate about certain things, and those things I did so well. And other things I wasn't passionate about, I didn't do as well. Unless it was forced upon me, then you could see my light shine through a little. So it was confusing for people. I often hear, "She's MORE than capable. It seems to be hit and miss, though. She must not want to be successful."

I can't even count how many times in my life I've had to apologize to people. Or how often I'm just on time or a few minutes late. I'm like that girl, with her ponytail half done. Maybe in pj's, running down the hallway to get her scrubs on and take that report just in the knick of time. Whether you believe it or not, I swear to you I'm trying, and I do have my best intentions in what I'm doing. Some days are just a bit more of a struggle.

Throughout this journey of learning about my ADHD and how it coincides with my personality traits. I've taken the time to recognize the advantages and disadvantages of my personality traits and how my ADHD affects or supports them. So I realize now I may not have told you exactly what I was diagnosed with. Three different types have categorized ADHD. Inattentive type, hyperactive-impulsive type, or combination type.

Inattentive: gets distracted easily, has poor concentration and organizational skills. Impulsivity: interrupts a lot and is a risk-taker. Hyperactivity: seems to always be on the go, talks a lot, maybe fidgety, and has difficulty staying on task. I have less hyperactive traits but can have trouble staying on task because I can get bored. I also can get fidgety for the same reason. You may catch me playing with something in my hand to keep my concentration higher. Mini Playdoughs have been a godsend, lol.

My biggest accomplishment as a teenager that let my ADHD SHINE was quitting school at age 16 (grade 11) because I got pregnant. At that time, my high school counselor told me that if I was deciding to be a mother, that had to be my priority and that school wasn't expected for someone in my situation.

I was fortunate enough to have a high school Principal who felt different about my abilities. She pushed forward to help people like myself and other moms get their butts back to school and allowed us to finish.

A new young mother daycare opened up on our school grounds that allowed me to come back in November of my proposed graduation year. I remember breastfeeding in between classes. I completed grades 11 and 12 in only eight months. I walked in that graduation ceremony with my nine-month baby on my hip, feeling oh so ever proud. I can thank my high school counselor, who didn't believe in me. Who did very little to help my success. As my catalyst to prove her wrong. Thank you for "oppositional defiance." Thank you, ADHD. Lol

I went on to enroll in my Bachelor Of Science in Nursing. I finished my Diploma in nursing (ended up having a second child halfway through, and my brother passed away), so I didn't quite finish my degree. I landed a job right away being an Emergency Room nurse and have been there for nearly 17 years.

You may now not be surprised to know halfway through my nursing career, I decided on a whim to purchase a commercial building. And opened a retail store selling athletic shoes/apparel, and it had a local real fruit smoothie bar! I was involved in all the local events. I supplied the town for many years with uniforms for our soccer teams. I held a small-town Weight Loss event a few years in a row. Oh yes, I also took a little adventure and went casual at the hospital while I tromped the Oil and Gas industry grounds and became a "Patch RN." Wow, how cool it was to be driving a 4X4 truck with a mini ambulance on the back and wearing steel-toe boots. Haha. It was an exciting time in my life, and it gave me a break in my life that I needed to keep passionate. From the outside, I won't lie; people didn't get it. I didn't get why I needed to do this. But I just did. And I was successful.

In the middle of Timbuktu, Canada, it was minus 50 Celcius. I had no one to talk with. My brain never stopped. I was taking courses and doing things online that interested me in between patients. Thankfully up north, most of my patients were healthy individuals, so my visits were far between. It was at that time I realized I was capable of more than just working in a hospital. And my passion for shoes was never really a thing. I recognized more of my need to be my own boss. I needed to be in a job that allowed me just to be me. Again, I did not know I had ADHD, but I knew I was different from most.

I came up with my fabulous business idea of becoming and owning a Nursing Patient Care Advocacy Company. I knew I had enough courage to speak up, I knew I thought very well outside the box, and that I could catch details that sometimes most people couldn't. I knew I had the passion for helping patients I felt were not having their voices heard with their healthcare teams. And sometimes, I knew they just didn't have the courage and wanted to help them find their courage or even be their voice.

In a medic truck, I created my business plan on a cold winter day in northern Alberta, wearing steel-toe boots and a cute stickered-up hard hat. I know what you may be thinking, should I not have been working? Yes, my supervisor was okay with me doing my own thing in between patients. My criteria from him, "I don't care if you sleep. I don't care if you watch NetFlix. Bring a pillow if you so desire. You just answer that radio when we need you. "Yes, best job ever except for the loneliness and isolation from family and people. But me being me. I entertained myself and my busy mind. I poured so much heart and soul into a business plan because I had no distractions. I created Nightingale Patient Care Advocacy Corp. I launched it in the fall of 2014.

Having my own business has allowed me to play with my creativity and cater my business to suit my needs and others. I have learned along the way, though, being an entrepreneur, I am just simply not good at certain things. Yet excellent at others. My pride got in the way a lot of the time, and I will not lie... it caused me to become stagnated in tasks that I was determined to "do myself."

I'm not always good at time management unless I already set out a schedule, plan, or list. I will often be late paying bills, not because I didn't have the money. But instead, I forgot to open my bank account and hit 'Pay.' Authorized payment plans have been a godsend, I believe for most. But especially for people like me.

So you can imagine how someone like this would find challenges in their life, with parenting, with a career, a business, and just living day to day. But, the upside is, regardless of not knowing I had ADHD, I still succeeded. I feel my life has been wonderful. I love parts of my ADHD and contribute a lot of my success to them. I continue to work on its traits that are not so desirable, and I keep getting better at it. Having the people, I love in my life know that I have made it easier for them to understand my challenges, and they can be a great support in helping me with specific tasks.

Now, let's talk about medication. It does help. It has side effects, and it is not for everyone. Ever since my diagnosis, I have tried different medications. I have learned what works and what doesn't. Do they help? Oh yes. Are there side effects? Usually yes. It's like taking your busy brain that may look from the outside a sea of squirrels running around, haha, and it pulls them in and has them all sitting down paying attention. I honestly only use it when I feel I need that extra dopamine to help concentrate. Particularly things maybe I find less than desirable.

I have learned to delegate tasks that I'm not so great at doing. AND accepting the fact it's easy to delegate things you're not good at... but accepting you also may have to delegate the things you are good at. But either don't want to do it or likely not going to do it. It was a tough one for me, and I won't lie. I'm a person who always feels if I can do it myself, I should. It was me, watching so many interviews of other ADHD entrepreneurs, that helped me realize that it was okay to do this. That I may be surprised how much more I accomplished by just doing this.

Meditating was another thing that I started to do in the last two years. Trust me, initially, when someone told me I should meditate, I was like, No way can this busy brain sit still long enough to meditate. I started with something called Tapping. I learned from a girlfriend who attended a business event. Wow, that was a game-changer for me. I took that and eventually incorporated ten minutes short meditations once a day and worked my way up. Why did this help? The wonders of finding different creative ways just to SLOW DOWN YOUR BRAIN.

Even if it's just ten minutes, it will do so many wonders for you. It allows things to start balancing. It slows the stress hormones. And, it does so much more. I will let the experts tell you what it does, but I promise everyone could find benefits.

Mindfulness has also been huge for me. I am being more mindful and learning more about cognitive distortions how anxiety works in my mind. They have all been great tools. When you realize that you are the creator of your own reality, it helps a lot.

Exercise! Wow.. this also was a game-changer. Yoga is wonderful—another form of meditation. Get out there. Move your body. Get your heart racing. I promise you if you have ADHD, it will only help big time. I recently lost 100 lbs during my big journey. I incorporated many things, and it's been a life-changing experience. I want people to take away from this if you have ADHD or may think you have it. Know that many successful people live with this. Own what your momma gave you and master it! I know that's my plan!

I want to share with you these ten tips that may help you if you have ADHD.

1. Write down your deadlines and put them in a calendar with an alarm.
2. If you can't do number one, delegate someone who will remind you.
3. Take frequent breaks while doing something that feels enjoyable. That little bit of excitement will raise your dopamine and help you get back on task.
4. If you are getting overwhelmed with projects: outsource!

5. Learn about mindfulness and try your best to maintain it. It will help you pay attention to your emotions and how they affect you and the reality around you.
6. Don't take on more than you can handle.
7. Consider medication if you can't manage your symptoms on your own
8. Exercise! I won't even begin to try and explain the benefits. You know them already.
9. Eat healthy, and just simply take care of your body. Remember your ADHD is neurological and is part of your body. So give it the best chance.
10. Seek counseling: there is so much to learn about ADHD, and there is more support now.

If you wish to be tested for ADHD, just ask your Family Doctor or counselor. There is a lot of help out there. The internet is full of resources that can help you. The most important thing is to be tested, and if you discover you have ADHD, well then now you know, and you can learn how to live your life with more peace.

Vannessa Fowler

Warrior Woman Alchemy
A JOURNEY FROM PAIN TO PEACE.

"Don't take for granted what you can do; don't be sloppy with your life. Devote life to a higher purpose: service to others. The warrior doesn't give up what they love. The warrior finds the love in what they do."
Dan Millman

I t was the summer of 2010, and I had just returned to my hometown of Fort St. John, BC, after several years of living in the Niagara, ON region. I had enjoyed the last few years of my life because it was new, exciting, and full of adventure, travel, music, and I became a bit of a free-spirited gypsy.

I had missed my family and friends over the years. As I was approaching 30, I decided to return for a short while to reconnect with everyone and figure out the next chapter of my life. Once I got settled in at my mom's place for a few days, I decided to go out and meet up with some old friends at our favorite pub, which always featured live music, one of my favorite things.

When I arrived, I caught up with some friends, and they introduced me to a handsome guy who was at their table. I remembered having a crush on him from high school. He had such a gorgeous smile and great energy about him. We hit it off right away, and over the next few months, we spent a lot of time together connecting over our love of music and the outdoors. We had long conversations about lots of interesting and intellectual things. We were both very artistic and passionate people and connected on a deeper level than I had with any partners in my past, and we fell in love! Then at the beginning of December, we decided that I would move in with him at his third-floor apartment in town.

I loved that we connected so well, we laughed a lot, and it felt easy to fall for him. We shared our love for music and outdoor adventures. He was super romantic and would sing and serenade me with his guitar while I soaked in the bathtub. We would have fun writing songs together and spent our days off hiking, fishing, and exploring. Everything was starting to feel like it was all falling into place, like a dream come true. It was December 9th, and we had just finished moving my things in a few days before, we had a trip planned that weekend, we had a nice dinner and decided to stay up late to watch "I'm Not There" a movie about Bob Dylan that he was excited for me to watch with him.

I was starting to fall asleep while watching the movie, so I let him know that I was going to crawl into bed. He said he was just going to stay up and watch the rest of the movie and would join me after. I woke up to him getting into bed around 5 am, and I remember reaching over, and he was still fully clothed with jeans on. I was very sleepy but remembered saying, "you should take your jeans off, babe, or you'll be uncomfortable," then I fell right back asleep.

A short time later, I woke up to him on top of me, touching and grabbing me aggressively, and then he began biting at my inner thighs and pelvic area, it was uncomfortable and painful, and I began to try and squirm away to get him to stop. The more I tried to get him to stop, the more persistent and aggressive he became. I tried speaking to him and telling him to stop, but he didn't. He wouldn't even respond to me and continued forcing himself on me. Something felt very off, his energy, the way he was not communicating, and the erratic and aggressive way he grabbed me. I was getting so scared.

He started to forcefully penetrate me as I was trying to get away, I remember grabbing and pushing the top of his head and shoulders in an attempt to get him off me, but he was too strong. This did not feel like the man I was in love with? This felt so scary! Why was he doing this to me? I finally shouted at him to stop, and was crying. I heard a noise, and he must've heard it too, it was a voice, it was my boyfriend in the living room... this was not my boyfriend doing this to me, this was someone else!

The man scrambled out of the bedroom, and all I could do was just cry and tremble. I knew I was in shock, and I was so scared. I could hear a commotion in the entryway and the sound of the door opening, and my boyfriend yelling. It turned out that my boyfriend fell asleep on the couch while trying to finish the movie and awoke to the sounds of me crying out. When he saw the man running towards the front door holding his pants up and grabbing his shoes, he leaped over the back of the couch to chase after him, but in the dark, he ran face-first into a moving dolly, and it sent him backward.

The man ran down the hallway of our floor towards the exit with my boyfriend chasing him, but he couldn't catch him after hitting the dolly, then he realized he didn't know if I was alright and came back to see if I was okay. I collapsed in his arms in the hallway outside of our bedroom and cried. I told him that I thought it was him coming to bed after the movie and didn't know why he was so aggressive; that's when we both realized the gravity of what just happened.

My boyfriend called 911, and the police arrived to question us about the intrusion. As I sat there trying to explain what happened, I could feel my whole body aching, shaking, and trembling. My entire sense of self, safety, and security had been violated. I felt stripped bare, raw, and alone. I felt like I couldn't even think straight; I was still confused about what happened, how it happened, and why. The police were so supportive, and the male constable must have known my sense of vulnerability and fear. He was very gracious, and I don't even know how to explain it, but the way he spoke to me and his mannerisms were comforting and allowed me to feel a sense of safety in discussing the incident and assured me that I was protected at that moment.

Once our initial statements were given, the officers told us they needed to dust our apartment for fingerprints and take all of our bedding for forensic testing. I needed to go to the hospital and have a "rape kit" done to swab for DNA, a Tetanus shot because of the bite wounds, and tests to ensure that this person had not transmitted any STDs to me as well. It was that word that really hit home and sunk into my stomach... I had been raped.

I was in the hospital room, alone with the female doctor examining me and collecting all of the samples she needed. I just stared up at the fluorescent lights in the ceiling listening to the hum. I had tears rolling down my cheeks, I felt numb, my body and soul felt so violated, and I began to completely disconnect from myself at that moment. I no longer wanted to be in my body.

Coming home to that apartment with fingerprint dust everywhere and our bedroom completely torn apart, I knew things were never going to be the same, and I didn't know if I was ever going to feel okay again. I was devastated. I was empty.

RCMP Victims Services began working with me to get counseling and other resources, but I didn't know how to carry on. They had the assailant's DNA, and my boyfriend had a vague description of the back of the person he saw running down the hallway because it was so dark neither of us saw his face; other than that, we had nothing to go on. The RCMP constable told me that unless the person has been arrested before or gets arrested in the future, they will not be able to find a DNA match. They suspected it was someone who knew me or was following me, and without having any leads or arrests, my sense of safety was non-existent.

To top it all off, my employer was not allowing me any more time off work because the busy Christmas season was upon us. I went back to work and had to face the public, customers coming in and me silently questioning if every man that walked up to my counter was him! I came home every day exhausted from having my guard up and constantly looking over my shoulder. I struggled when alone. I didn't want to eat, and I struggled to drive, grocery shop, sleep or even shower with the curtain closed despite the door being locked.

Every night I struggled when I tried to fall asleep, I would have panic attacks, and my body would tense. I was terrified to close my eyes. When I did eventually succumb to the exhaustion, I would have horrific nightmares. Several reoccurring ones of a large faceless man standing in the doorway to my bedroom making disturbing noises, or a horned demon man crawling up my legs from the bottom of the bed grasping at my pelvic and abdomen area with claws on his hands. I would wake up flailing, screaming, with my heart racing, petrified and crying, and these night-mares went on for months.

In the new year, we moved to a different place, and I left my job for an office position where I didn't have to face the public. I continued weekly counseling. I had multiple other experiences of unspeakable violence and trauma that caused me to disassociate from my body and gave me over-whelming feelings of worthlessness. I knew my boyfriend carried the guilt of not being able to stop the assault, and I could tell it was starting to affect him and our relationship together. We each had our own struggles of grief and trauma, and a little over a year later, our relationship ended.

I was determined to continue my healing process and do what I needed to get through this. I had many days where I struggled and suffered from the pain of what happened. I didn't know if I would ever heal, feel safe, whole, or connected to my body again. That's when I began my yoga journey.

I desperately needed to feel a sense of connection and community after feeling so alone and isolated for so long. I began practicing yoga at a female-owned and operated studio in town. I actually knew the owner from school, and she always made me feel like I was in a safe space and supported when I practiced with her.

Day by day, week by week, and month by month, I felt stronger and more connected to my body through breath, movement, mantra, and stillness. There were days I would cry during or after practice because the emotions I had been bottling up started to release every time I was held in the sense of a safe community. These experiences allowed for the deepest healing within me, and I knew it was my time to start taking my power back.

The local Women's Resource Society hosts an annual walk to "Take Back The Night" through the downtown core. They protest gender-based violence and stop at landmarks throughout the city where assaults on women are most likely to happen. I decided to volunteer and get involved. I didn't want any other women to go through what I did. If there were anything I could do to help, I would.

So, I decided to use my voice. I wrote my speech, a story of the violence I experienced in my life and how I've been overcoming it. On the night of the march, we rallied outside one of the strip clubs where violence has occurred. It was the first stop on our march through the city, and it was my turn; I was up. I stood there in the street, voice shaking, nerves bundling up, tears forming in my eyes, lights, cameras, and eyes of people on me, and I told my story.

This was one of the most profound and empowering moments of my healing journey, to no longer carry the shame, silence, and guilt of what happened to me, and to speak it out loud for everyone to hear, that man suddenly felt powerless to me, a weak, sad human. In fact, I began to have compassion for him because whatever that person experienced in life, to do that to another human means he was suffering more than I was. I had become strong because I took my traumas and used them to strengthen myself and, in turn, used my voice to speak up for those who couldn't.

After the march, I was approached in person and online by several victims and family members telling me that my story empowered them to come forward, work harder at protecting their loved ones, and speak out more against violence. A young man, only 12 years old, was so moved he came and asked if he could hug me. He said he was so sorry that happened to me and that he will do everything he can in his life to make sure none of the women he knows has to go through what I did. He cried and hugged me. Another was a beautiful woman who had experienced a trauma-tizing home intrusion and sexual assault. She was tormented by her assailant and split from her fiancé after-ward. This woman hadn't told anyone else what happened or what she went through, and she said my story, and the fact that I spoke about it and took steps towards healing helped her see that she had the strength to heal also. (I am happy to say that she and I still talk, and she has done an immense amount of healing and is thriving in her life now as well.)

My involvement with the Women's Resource Society was rewarding and helped me find strength, but I knew that I still had healing to do. Knowing that my voice and story gave others the power to help and heal themselves was all the fuel I needed to keep going. I knew that I had come through the worst of it, and if I can continue to do the work to heal and empower myself, I can continue to help others.

It was then that I decided that I would finally move forward with the next chapter of my journey as I had planned to do when I got back to my hometown. I booked my tickets, packed my bags, and headed to Nepal for the next phase of my healing and to grow myself and my knowledge of self-acceptance, self-love, and self-healing through yoga, mantra, ritual, and meditation.

There was something so exciting, invigorating, and calming about knowing I was embarking on a solo adventure halfway across the world, stepping entirely out of my comfort zone and putting everything I had into my personal growth and healing.

I was in Nepal for six months. The first two months were spent in intensive yoga teacher training, where I discovered an even deeper level of stored trauma. And my teachers, at one point, questioned whether or not someone with my level of violent trauma, especially so recent, was ready to go on an already emotional journey of deeper yogic tradition and lifestyle learning.

I persisted and told them I take full responsibility for myself and everything that comes up as we go through the deeper levels of practice. I knew I had to get there. I had to devote myself to this with all of my heart because I didn't want to carry this burden anymore. And if I got super emotional, messy, painful, and violently ill in the process, I was ready and willing to deal with that!

And yes.. all of that and more happened. Some days were incredibly painful, horrible, disgustingly sickening, and devastating, like experiencing it all over again and then some. Then the purge of it all, physically and emotionally regurgitating all of it out of my mind, body, and soul, it was one hell of an experience!

I walked out of my yoga teacher training with an appreciation for and connection to my body again, a love for myself that I have never felt before, a newfound respect for all that I am capable of; I know that I am in control of my thoughts. My mind has the power to heal my heart and my spirit. Since that last day of my training, I have a mantra that I tell myself daily and even include in my classes when I teach: I give thanks to my body for its mobility, to my mind for its strength, to my breath for its life, and to my heart for its light.

I am emotional now, just reflecting on it. It took an immense amount of strength and fortitude to get me through the healing from those 2.5 years of my life, and nobody will ever truly know and understand what it was like but me, and that's okay because I did what I felt needed to be done.

After my yoga training, I spend the next four months traveling across Nepal, meeting locals, connecting with other travelers. I lived in cities and remote villages, trekking deep into several areas of the Himalayas and allowing myself to just exist and experience life in my body with this newfound appreciation.

There was one part of my adventure in particular that stands out to me. The almost exact moment that I knew, and felt in my whole being, that all I went through, what I did, and my journey of healing, was what I had to do if I wanted to help others.

I decided to take the path less traveled and go to an area of Nepal that was not visited as much as other areas. I wanted to be around as few people as possible, let myself be surrounded by the majesty and power of these ancient mountains, powerful rivers, and dense jungle to allow my journey to sink in.

I took a full-day bus ride out of Kathmandu to a remote village where I would begin my trek on foot. The road leading up to the village was treacherous, and at times I couldn't even see the ground beneath us as I looked out the window staring down to the cliffs below. I heard stories of landslides and ground giving way and swallowing buses and other vehicles down the mountain; as scary as that was, I did my best just to trust that this was not the end of the road for me. I had more work to do in this life.

I arrived at the village, and the next morning started my ascent to the towering giants above me. The Himalayas are the absolute most stunning things I have ever laid my eyes upon. By this point, I had already explored and trekked several other areas of the mountains. Still, this one was especially important to me because of its connection to Tibet, the vastness of the wilderness, and lack of human traffic. I trekked for seven days, through dense jungle, over raging rivers, through beautiful alpine valleys filled with wildflowers, around cliffs, over very rickety suspension bridges, and finally to the base of the rocky mountainside where the snow and glaciers lived above.

On the 7th day of hiking, I reached the base of this mountain, where one of the oldest Tibetan monasteries in the region is. No monks were living there anymore, and the building was very old. There was one older monk who has stayed over the years as a caretaker. He did not speak any English but motioned for me to stay and meditate with him. Afterward, we went to the home where I was to spend the night, and the woman who lived there spoke very little English, but she has a small homestead and a yak. I paid her for my sleeping quarters, a bucket of cold water to bathe in, and some freshly made Buckwheat pancakes with yak curd (yogurt). I rested my bones for the night, it was a very long week to get here, and I knew I still had a lot more to do and explore.

The next day I set out and hiked up the glacier valley, through a herd of yak's and their babies in their summer grazing territory, over the streams and rivers to the frozen peaks above. I hiked for hours and didn't come across a single person that day, and when I reached a small peak facing the towering glacier above me, I stopped. I sat there in awe of the mountain in front of me and reflected on my journey to get there; the trauma, violence, pain, struggle, heartbreak, fear, loss, healing, acceptance, love, gratitude, and new life!

Looking around me at the vastness of my surroundings and breathing in all of the steps of my journey, I felt deep within my heart that this path of mine, as painful as it was, the blood, sweat, tears, every step was worth it to get me to this breathtaking place. This was my reward for all the work I had done, and this was the most amazing gift. This was my life.

I realized that I was healing because I faced adversity. I did the most painful and uncomfortable things that I didn't want to do. I let my voice be heard, and I learned how to move through fear. I sat in hours of stillness and meditation, and I cried, I chanted mantras hundreds and thousands of times, I breathed through the pain and trusted that on the other side of it all was something so much greater than I could imagine.

I felt a deep inner peace at that moment, and the tranquility washed over me like a warm, soothing wave. I took a deep inhale, and a long, slow, cleansing exhale. I felt my shoulders drop, and my face softened, the corners of my mouth turned upward to a smile. A tear trickled down my cheek, and the mountain breeze gently blew my hair off my neck as I held my head up high. I remember all the precious details of this moment because it's the moment that I knew that I was no longer strong because I had endured. I am strong because I did everything in my power to rise up!

This day. This moment. This heartbeat. This breath. This is the first - of the rest and best of my life!

Love & Gratitude
Anne-Marie Harris

4

Resiliency and Resolution
HOW I FOUGHT FOR A DIAGNOSIS AND
TREATMENT

"Don't let fear keep you quiet. You have a voice so use it. Speak up. Raise your hands. Shout your answers. Make yourself heard. Whatever it takes, just find your voice, and when you do, fill the damn silence."
Meredith Grey

"**M**ommy, did you change your tampon?" my four-year-old asked as I snuggled beside her to cuddle her to sleep. This may seem like a strange question, but this becomes standard when you have menstrual bleeding every day for over a year. Sadly, our cuddles have been cut short more times than I'd like to remember because I've suddenly had to rush to the washroom.

I had always felt comfortable standing up for myself, but when 2018 started, I didn't realize how hard I would have to fight. I grew up naive. I'm a white female living in Canada; perhaps I chose to believe what I wanted. Statistics have shown that women of color face much more challenging obstacles regarding their health, specifically their reproductive health. While I was aware of these statistics, my own ignorance was coming into play.

I had always thought when something was wrong, you went to the doctor, and they would fix it. They would run all tests and explore all options and find the cause. My obsession with Grey's Anatomy could have also brought on this naivety. It turns out I was wrong. Very wrong.

When it comes to women's health, it is also dismissed and shrugged off. Between May 31, 2018, and June 6, 2019, there was a combined 44 days I didn't have menstrual bleeding. I will share what happened, what I felt I did right, and what I wish I had done.

Around October of 2017, my period started getting heavier; I started tracking it as that progressed. I had gone to walk-in clinics, and they told me that I was having a miscarriage. Now I found this hard to believe because I took my birth control daily, and the bleeding started when it should as per my pills. It also didn't seem likely that a woman who wasn't trying to get pregnant got pregnant two months in a row and miscarried on the exact day her period was due. In hindsight, at this point, I should have gone to my doctor. I eventually went to my doctor, who referred me to an OBGYN I had previously seen for IUDs.

When I first saw my new OBGYN, she didn't do any tests but did prescribe a new birth control pill and Tranexamic acid (TXA). Different birth control pills have a different makeup of estrogen and progesterone to balance your hormones and prevent pregnancy. The new birth control was another hormonal makeup that my OBGYN was hopeful would stop whatever was going on. TXA is a drug commonly used to slow uterine bleeding. May 31, 2018, I got my period...and it didn't stop.

After a few weeks, it still hadn't stopped. I spent months bleeding with zero tests being done except to check my ferritin and hemoglobin. I asked for biopsies and ultra-sounds and was told no. I was never given a reason as to why they didn't want to. I've always been someone who needs to understand the big picture, and I couldn't wrap my head around why she was throwing medication at something she hadn't even diagnosed yet. I had asked about endometriosis, a cyst, and others, and they were all ruled out due to my symptoms. My doctor explained endometriosis would cause constant pain, and I wasn't in constant pain. I was only in pain when I passed a clot. If things are ruled out, why are we not looking for the problem before finding a solution?

The first time I stood up for myself was when the pain and bleeding were unbearable, and I went to the emergency. I saw a doctor, and by chance, my OBGYN was there. The doctor working in the emergency room was kind and comforting. The ER doctor, my OBGYN, and I all agreed that if it hadn't gotten better in two days to come back, they would do a D&C to see if that helped. I went back two days later, and they told me they would do the surgery, and while I waited for an OR, they would do an iron infusion as my ferritin and hemoglobin were low. This was perfect. Then in a blink of an eye, they were trying to send me home. It was like one of those scenes where you are frozen, and everything is zipping around you. I said no. I would not go home; they would be doing the surgery.

The doctors advised me that my OBGYN told them to have me come the next day so she could do it. I swear I saw red. Why would you ask me to come back in two days, not three? Why would you waste my time and the time of the staff at the hospital? I told them no. Whoever was on-call would. That wasn't an option as I had a local OBGYN. I felt awful for the poor intern who was taking the brunt of my anger. The poor intern went from giving me hope to ripping it away from me. What you need to understand is I'm not someone who takes things lying down. I won't go down without a fight.

I told them, okay, I was firing her, and there I no longer had an OBGYN, and the on-call had to see me. I thought if I fired her, they would have to get the oncall to see me. They told me this wasn't the case, and if I decided to fire my OBGYN, I would have to get a new referral. The doctor I had seen a few days prior and my OBGYN came in about an hour later. They told me that the doctor I had seen earlier that day told both of them I refused to let my OBGYN see me and that I wouldn't let her touch me with a 10foot pole. None of this was true. Needless to say, by the end of the day, I finally got my surgery.

For a few weeks, the bleeding stopped. When my period came, I was terrified. What if it didn't stop again? That fear came true, and it didn't stop. I went to see my OBGYN, and she gave me three options:

- Hysterectomy
- Uterine Ablation
- Do nothing, and hopefully, it stops.

Excuse me, what? You haven't even done an ultrasound, and you want to remove my uterus? You have to be kidding me. You don't even know what is causing this. She never gave me a clear answer on why she didn't want to do an ultrasound. The most frustrating part was later learning that her clinic had an ultrasound machine there, and she still didn't want to do one. The D&C was performed in the hospital by the on-call doctor. He noted that there was a thickening of my uterus. When I asked my doctor for clarification on what that meant, she shrugged and said it happens.

I got a second opinion. I went back to my family doctor and explained what had been going on and what options were suggested by the first OBGYN he had sent me to. He was absolutely floored. I had gone to my family doctor for advice throughout the summer when I couldn't reach my OBGYN. He had prescribed progesterone to stop the bleeding. While it wouldn't stop the issue, it would give me a temporary break from the bleeding I so desperately needed. I told him that a hysterectomy had been suggested, and being in my early 30s, this was a big decision, and I wanted a second opinion. I asked to be sent to Dr. Benoit.

Before all of this, I had also lost two pregnancies. When I lost the second, I didn't have a doctor covering my pregnancy, and Dr. Benoit happened to be on-call. Dr. Benoit performed more tests on me after that second pregnancy loss than you can imagine. He did so many blood tests one day that they had told me to have someone drive me home because I wouldn't be able to, and they were not wrong.

Due to our history, I knew I could trust him, and he would look for answers. The first thing he did was send me for an ultrasound. Within three weeks of our initial visit, we had an answer. Fibroids. I had three fibroids that were causing my bleeding. It was that simple. A simple ultrasound solved a mystery that had consumed my life for months.

I thought this was the start of having hope. I was wrong. The fight wasn't over. Obviously, he wanted me to get them removed, but I couldn't afford to take six weeks off work. So we decided that I would get on a waitlist to have them removed laparoscopically. There was hope.

Without getting into too many graphic details, the bleeding got much, much worse. The long and short of it is one day was impossibly bad. I remember laying on the bench watching my daughter's swim lesson, then as we drove to Wal-Mart, having to hold onto the seat belt to stop me from moving. When we got to Wal-Mart, it was the worst it had ever been. There was so much blood, and the clots were larger than you could imagine. They say to go to the hospital if your clots are bigger than a toonie; mine couldn't be held in two hands. I was crying and shaking. This is one of the worse memories that I have so vividly. I cleaned up the washroom the best I could and had to tell a Walmart employee what had happened and apologized. I found my husband and daughter and had to use the cart for support because I was so weak that I couldn't keep myself up, and I was in so much pain. My daughter was seated in the cart and kept leaning over to hug me and say it's okay. It broke my heart. I was the parent, not her, and she shouldn't have to take care of me.

We got home, where I passed more clots. Being as Dr. Benoit works at a fertility clinic, they did have an email. I was able to send him pictures of the clots; yes, I took pictures. I still remember that night sitting in the bath, holding my knees sobbing. I didn't know if this would ever end or if this was my life now. I knew that worst-case scenario, I could always get a hysterectomy, and that would solve the problem, but in the moment when you're that scared and in that much pain, those facts don't register. Despite everything, that day and those clots are still the most vivid and terrifying memory.

The next day (Monday), Dr. Benoit's office called me to come in right away. Dr. Benoit had seen the photos, and even though it was his day off, he wanted to see me.

Plain and simple, we needed to make the bleeding stop. It was now December, but it wouldn't be until January that I had extended health. They happened to have an extra IUD they were willing to give me for free, and they wanted me to take an insane amount of birth control as well. I'm taking two pills three times a day. When you get an IUD, they use a tool to measure your uterus to see how far to insert it. When mine was measured, it was 11cm, a normal uterus is 7cm. This was due to the fibroids. They had made my uterus that much larger, which also explained why I bled so much. There was more space and more lining to be shed.

The bleeding slowed down but didn't stop. In January, I started Lupron. Lupron is a chemotherapy drug used to treat prostate cancer. What it does is essentially turns off your hormones. Fibroids grow off estrogen, so by turning that off, it would shrink and stop bleeding. Many people had asked why I didn't start Lupron when I had severe bleeding at Walmart? Lupron is about $800 a month without extended health, so we had to wait.

Well, low and behold, my bleeding still didn't stop. At about month 4 of Lupron and still bleeding, we decided to remove my IUD. It isn't common to have an IUD while getting Lupron, and we wondered if that's why I was still bleeding.

It wouldn't come out. No matter how hard the doctor pulled, it would not come out. I nearly passed out. He had a laparoscopy in his office, and we decided the following week I would take an Ativan, and he would use the camera to see what was going on.

You have no idea how cool it is to see inside your body on a monitor. It is beyond cool! Then he said, "hmmm, interesting." Typically you don't want to hear that from a doctor who has a camera inside your body. But there it was. My fibroid. It wasn't in the muscular tissue of my uterus as most are. It was right there. This meant three things.

My IUD was just stuck behind it and would not come out easily with the guidance of my doctor.

This is why the bleeding never stopped. I didn't need super invasive surgery. I just needed a really aggressive D&C.

Now the disappointing part of this was Dr. Benoit didn't have hospital privileges. He is was older and wanting to retire. You need to be on-call a certain amount to have hospital privileges, and he didn't want to do that anymore. He requested all my notes to another OBGYN he knew, assuming that I would be taken in fairly quickly.

I was not.

I called to follow up, and they said that it would be three to six months before I would be able to come in for a consult, and from there, they would schedule surgery.

I couldn't wait that long. You can only be on Lupron for six months at a time, which would put me outside of that. While the Lupron hadn't stopped the bleeding, it slowed it down substantially. All the hair loss, skin burns, weight gain, and other terrible side effects would be for nothing. What I endured for Lupron couldn't be a waste. I couldn't go off it and have everything come back just as it was before.

I remember sitting in my office bawling. How could this be happening? The surgery was simple. Why wouldn't they see me? I was so frustrated. I wasn't sad or defeated. I was mad and frustrated. I couldn't yell or scream, so I cried. I let myself cry for ten minutes and pulled myself together, and went on with my day. As mad as I was, I couldn't let this news consume my day. I still had an office to run and a family to enjoy.

A week or so after finding that out, I was at work, and everything started to spin, and I didn't know where I was. It wasn't a sense of confusion but closer to a dissociated episode. My co-worker took me to the emergency room, where it was determined I had gone into shock. My ferritin and hemoglobin were so low that my body went into shock. I had the hospital send my hospital report to my new OBGYN. I called again, and they said my situation was not "urgent or serious," and I could expect a call in about four months.

At this point, I started calling every single OBGYN I could find online and plead with them. All had similar wait times, and none thought I was important. Granted, I was talking to the receptionist. They didn't know my case, and the doctors hadn't reviewed my file either.

I called Dr. Benoit in tears. He agreed this wasn't right and didn't understand why they wouldn't listen to him about how badly I needed this done. When I asked my family doctor to refer me to Dr. Benoit, my doctor wrote a long letter explaining how severe my case was. Dr. Benoit did the same when he sent out my referral. To have this ignored didn't seem right. Since no OBGYN in my area was going to take my case seriously, I told him I was willing to travel, and like that, he sent me to a neighboring town.

I was sent to see Dr. Procyshen, and oh my, is she amazing. She saw how important it was and was so kind and so compassionate. One thing she was worried about was whether it was cancerous. She was concerned because of how rapidly it had grown. We scheduled my surgery for three weeks, and I was set. As relieved as I was, I did feel bad; she moved a cesarean for me. To whoever that was, I'm very sorry. The cancer fear was still there, but it was going to be removed.

On the day of surgery, my husband and daughter came with me. I held my daughter so tight. It was a simple procedure, but the idea of not waking up broke my heart. I couldn't leave her. This entire time I hadn't been scared. Annoyed and frustrated, yes, scared no. Surgery always scares me. What if you don't wake up? While going under, I started coughing really bad, and that was terrifying. I woke up and was told everything went well. I recovered at my mom's, and my husband came and got me the next day. If you're wondering why I recovered there, my mom lives in the town I had surgery, so it was easier.

After that, my periods were normal. I could not believe it. So much of my life had been consumed by this, and now it had stopped. And the biopsy? Totally benign!

During all this, I realized a lot of things. A big one was who was truly there for me. I had one friend who completely ghosted me. I never heard from her. She didn't ask how my surgery went, nothing. She was supposed to be one of my best friends, and she didn't seem to care. We have since mended that relationship and moved forward, but it did take some time.

I had other friends who went above and beyond. Despite how gross it was, they were there. She is not someone who ever discusses feelings or medical problems, so to have her be there and hide any ounce of being uncomfortable was beyond words to me. When I had surgery, she called and texted my parents non-stop to see what was going on.

Some family would tell me how disgusting it was and how no one wanted to hear it. In those moments, I realized what I actually meant to them. I understood that, yes, it was uncomfortable, but they heard the bare minimum details about it. My parents did the best they could with it. I didn't tell them how bad it was, how much I was struggling mentally, and how much I needed them. I didn't want to burden them or scare them. I should have been more honest with them. I've always been the person people go to when they need help, and a part of me thought that if I started to reach out for emotional support, they wouldn't feel comfortable coming to me when they needed help. As hurt as I was, some didn't proactively ask me how I was doing. I couldn't blame them as I never told them how severe it was or how I was feeling.

I also realized what a remarkable husband and daughter I had. My ferritin and hemoglobin were so low that I slept from 4 pm to 5 pm every day after work. I slept in the truck if we drove more than 15 minutes at a time. Adam did everything. He took care of our daughter and me. He held me when I needed it and made me laugh.

My daughter showed me how truly resilient kids are. Even at four, she knew something was wrong but never seemed scared. She loved me. We played, we cuddled, and she gave me hope. I needed to be the mom she deserved. Emily is the single most important thing to me (yes, my husband knows this as well), and to see her be brave was a gift I didn't know I needed.

A lot of people will ask me what it was like to be in constant pain and fear. It's very simple. I wasn't. The only time I was in pain was when I would pass a clot. My lady bits would sometimes start to ache from constantly changing tampons, but it wasn't a constant pain. I also wasn't scared. I knew that need be, we do a hysterectomy, and the bleeding would stop. A hysterectomy is final. I have one daughter who desperately wants a sibling. However, I want to keep this option open for her; if needed, I would have done the hysterectomy.

Another thing I discovered was how resilient I was. At the time, I ran a health clinic specializing in long-term disability cases where they would learn about resiliency. I never considered myself that tough or resilient. I was just doing what needed to be done. Whenever people would say, "you're so brave" or "how do you do it?" I would shrug and say I just do. Resiliency is defined as the capacity to recover quickly from difficulties; toughness. I may not have seen resiliency in myself, but others did, and if I'm honest, that felt nice.

What I discovered that I now warn other women about is your reproductive health will not be taken seriously. You will have to fight. Track EVERYTHING. I tracked the flow and clot size. I had copies of this on hand for doctors. I took pictures of everything to show how bad it was. Was this gross? Yes.

Some tips for tracking I want to share:

1. Get a journal or daytimer you love. What you are tracking is going to suck, so putting it in a book you don't enjoy always makes it harder.
2. Create a ledger so you don't have to write everything out every single time.
3. Take photocopies with you. The doctor may say no if you ask if they would like a copy, but you can leave it with them if you have it printed and ready.
4. If you have access to an online portal for your health, make sure you are using it to additionally track things.
5. Write down questions and write down answers.

A lot changed when I went through this. Now whenever someone posts in any group with women about menstrual problems, I am tagged. Even if the problem is different, the road to getting a diagnosis and treatment is not. I have spoken at Virtual Women Summits and have met with people one on one. I have never been a shy person. I have always been very open and will always welcome anyone who is struggling and needs guidance.

No one will fight harder for you than you will. It is an incredibly long and hard road, and you can do it.

Samantha Trarback

5

Mizpah
UNTIL WE MEET AGAIN

**"Sometimes you have to experience what you don't want
in life to come to a full understanding of what you do
want."**
The Mind's Journal

I don't remember much about that night. I only know
what people told me... and I was humiliated by what
they had to say.

Some friends and I were out celebrating that night as my
husband waited at home for me. We were having a great
time, laughing, telling stories, and drinking at a local bar. I
remember the beginning of the night, and I was having a
great time. By the end of it, though, I guess I had consumed
an unknown quantity of alcohol, threw up all over the bar,
was poured into someone's car, and carried into my house.

Apparently, I continued to throw up everywhere, stopped breathing, and nearly died that night, but the details to me were vague.

My poor husband bore the brunt of it all that night. He anxiously watched as the EMS went to work on me. He could only stand by and pray for the best outcome. I would come to severely regret the heartache I placed on him that night and many nights previous to that -- phone calls of friends telling him to come to get me from a bar.

I never did ask him to recall the specific details of that night to me, primarily due to shame, but also, I just thought it best not to know. I could beat myself up enough without knowing the intimate details.

Three days after, I felt human again. I got out of bed, looked around my house, and saw remnants of throw-up here and there. I peered in my purse, threw my head back in disgust, and eventually disposed of most of its contents. As I sat there contemplating, I was flooded with emotional tidal waves of shame and guilt. Hauntings of graphic details of the alcoholic demise of my father and grandfather before him filled my head. I couldn't be the third generation of people who dies from this disease. Profound sadness then overtook me, and I hung out there for a while.

What the hell was I doing with my life? I was only 40 years old. I couldn't die now. I sobbed uncontrollably and then made a decision—I gotta stop this madness, this constant cycle of burying pain in liquor and then paying the emotional price afterward. It is a vicious way to live. This life-altering decision to stop drinking was my pivotal moment, my exodus, my release from the bondage of booze. It had to be. I just had to seize the opportunity the universe was presenting me. I still wanted to live.

Once I decided to stop drinking, I felt like the clouds had separated from the sky, and a single beam of sunlight shone on me. That glorious feeling was short-lived because I knew I had some serious baggage I would have to tackle on my road to recovery. I needed to take a painful look at the past to begin to understand what led to this and its formation. I had to figure out what caused the disease and what perpetuated it and then learn lessons from it and grow. I felt to heal, and I had to understand my past, forgive it, and move forward. My journey to enlightenment started with looking back at my father, mother, childhood, and all the boxes I'd have to unpack.

My father and his family were immigrants from Europe who came here when he was a young teen. They settled in central Canada in the 1950s with the promise of work and new opportunities. His father found work in a factory and his mother in a hospital. Although he spoke the language, he had many other cultural obstacles, I am sure. Their home was in a less affluent area of the city, but nonetheless well kept.

I was told he ran away as a teen. Apparently, he jumped on a train and rode it out west. I am not entirely sure of what he ran away from, but it must have been awful in his mind. His father was an alcoholic too and ruled with a heavy, often violent hand. This may be where my dad learned how to discipline his children.

He later joined the US military and became a cop, a homicide detective to be exact once back on Canadian soil. He was brilliant and very witty, well-loved, and respected by his colleagues.

I know he saw some pretty gruesome scenes throughout his career, things he would probably want to forget. Maybe part of his drinking was done to do just that. Forget. I would later come to adopt this as a coping mechanism too. Booze was an excellent tonic for that.

His drinking destroyed his family. My mother left, and my sibling and I become conflictingly estranged. I felt alone and obligated to take care of him in his illness. I had the naivety of thinking I could move back into his house, make him stop drinking, and thereby save him. Those times represent some dark days in my life and led me down a dangerous path of fear, anxiety, and much counseling later on.

His untimely death was a long, painful, memorable experience. My dad was in the ICU for about six to eight weeks on a ventilator. I went to see him every single day. Up until the day the doctors finally had the family meeting with us, I really did think he was going to wake up. They told us it was time, though. His organs were all failing due to the years of alcohol abuse. What a gut punch that was. The life-ending responsibility fell on me as I was the next of kin. I remember thinking to myself, 20 years ago, he decided to give me life, and now I have to decide on his. That was anguishing. As I write this now so many years later, it is cathartic to think I am currently the age he was when he died. I wouldn't be ready to go now in the prime of my life at 50 years old.

The other parent in our home lived in denial and was seemingly complicit in the environment. I'd like to think she knew the abuse was all wrong but maybe felt powerless to change or challenge it? I guess I will never know. She died a long time ago, too, and I will never get an answer to "why didn't you stop it?". Later in life, she told me he wasn't violent towards her, just us, his defenseless kids. My mind justifies this flippantness by realizing it was a different time back then. The seventies and early eighties weren't as understanding to women wanting to be independently minded, especially towards their husbands. As a young adult, she would tell me she never wanted to leave him because of the kids. That explanation always really disappointed me. No guilt there.

Whenever there was conflict or issues with my mother, I always felt the need to process the situation by talking. I felt if we could just talk about it, we could work it out and feel better. I wanted to be expressive with my emotions. Her solution was just to bury and forget. She would always say, "I don't want to talk about it." Another reinforcement method of dealing with pain; forget and bury. Avoidance instead of dealing with problems is what I was taught to do. Alcohol became a cemetery of burials for me; way easier than confronting.

I don't blame my parents for my problems, but I see them as ignitors to a battle brewing in me. I am an adult now. I am responsible for my decisions and how I live my life, but

I can't escape my past. It is part of me, and I can't forget it. I know I have to learn from it, though, and forgive it. That's the hard part. Although the bruises have long healed, the emotional scars still live in the shadows of my mind and, unfortunately, are still easily stirred to this day.

When I was young, I always knew my father drank. He would come home from work, pour himself drink after drink, and often sit in the basement and watch sports or the news. I didn't realize that was a problem then. I just thought it was normal. I saw him drunk many times. When he was with friends, he was very humorous and witty. When they left, and the party was over, he sometimes got really angry. My sibling and I were easy targets. I was often terrified of him.

At school, I always told my classmates the belt marks on my legs were a result of me falling into a bush. My mother's voice echoed firmly in my head, "don't tell anyone what goes on in this house." Probably my most agonizing childhood experience happened in the girl's change room before gym class one day. I think I was in grade three or four. This vivid experience was more traumatic than the actual abuse and still plagues me to this day. One of my friends looked at me and asked what was on the back of my legs. I spouted out my automatic response, "Oh, I fell in a bush." There were only nine or ten girls in our class, and one, in particular, was very unpopular. Everyone picked on her. When she heard my auto-response, she lowered her head, looked straight at me, squinted her eyes, furrowed her brow, and said, "those are belt marks" in a low, poignant voice.

My visceral reaction was anger, but really this just masked my massive embarrassment. I vehemently denied it out loud in front of my friends, "No, it's not!!!...I fell." Later in my private time, I was deeply saddened because I knew she knew what the belt was too. (if you happen to read this, I want you to know I am so sorry). I couldn't afford to look uncool in front of my friends. Nor admit to the abuse I'd endured or even worse to sympathize with her in front of them. I was angry at the time in an unenlightened way. I also later wondered if she knew the feeling of throbbing head pain of being thrown up the stairs by your hair.

My kid brain did not know how to deal with this event and its precursors. I couldn't take this home with me and talk it out there. When we got home, we were programmed to forget. I didn't have understanding friends, and the culture back then was not supportive of interfering in the homes of families or expressing emotion.

There was no kids helpline or understanding school counselor. THERE WAS NO OUTLET when I needed so desperately to talk about this, so I suffered in silence and dealt with things the only way my juvenile mind knew how. I mimicked the way my father relieved his stress and forgot his problems. I drank…. I drank to forget. And so it started, the early evolution of my disease. I was drinking to bury, drinking to forget. Complacency eventually set in, and temporarily things became easier.

My childhood experiences taught me things, many of which I am sure were unintended. Fear being number one. Fear of everything. Fear of trying new things, fear of older men, and fear of speaking up led to a severe lack of confidence and some terrible decisions. I also missed quite a number of opportunities by way of this crippling fear. My life might have been very different if I had confidently pursued early childhood aspirations. I don't regret where my life is now, but it would probably have been quite different.

I also had difficulty forming relationships, both romantic and platonic. I always found it so awkward, and I didn't always know how to act. I constantly questioned everything I did and said over and over in my mind. I was so obsessed with what people thought of me. At the time, my secret weapon was booze. I could be open, carefree, and confident when I was drunk with aftereffects be damned. But then my inevitable hungover state slapped me back into reality, usually with a terrible emotional vengeance.

They say that time heals all wounds. I believe that to be somewhat accurate. I think as I have aged, some things have faded quite a bit. I have forgiven numerous things in the past, but mostly because they just happened so long ago, and I guess it is just not important anymore. Some things I have let go. Others are branded in my brain forever. Like that day in the change room or the pee your pants feeling from hearing the belt coming out of the closet heading for your virginal skin. I guess some things I will never forget or forgive.

I have been sober for a little over ten years now. It started the day after my last drunk, the night I almost died. This was the beginning of the awakened part of my life. No drinking anymore was eye-opening. So many things were different. I lost some friends. Correction, I had to lose some friends. I had to change some routines and activities, and I had to mourn some losses. Somehow by the grace of what I call the universe, I never got seriously injured, arrested, or physically injured someone else. Maybe in spirit, my dad was seeking atonement by looking out for me.

For me, the most powerful tool in maintaining my sobriety was what I called "seeing through to the consequences." When I was drinking, I did not care about tomorrow. Tomorrow didn't matter. I gave no thought to what I had to do or even whether I'd be able to make it to work. I didn't care that I would feel like shit the next day because I was having fun right now at the moment. There were no worries in the right now. All that mattered was when I was going to get my next drink. That lifestyle becomes very tiresome after a while.

To stay sober, I had to see the value of the consequence. There is no learning unless there is the realization of consequence. For me, the consequence had to be some type of sufferance or some kind of penalty. I had to realize that I could avoid that penalty if I just eliminated its source. I didn't want to wake up feeling like raw sewage anymore. I wanted to feel clear and healthy. I wanted what other sober people had.

I knew I couldn't be like those lucky people that could just have one drink and say, OK, that's it. For me, one is too many, and a thousand is not enough. I had to sever it, mourn it, and put it away forever. To this day, do I wish that I could just go out and have a glass of wine with the girls? Of course, I do. But I know that is impossible for me. I tell myself this is just something that I don't do anymore. I have to honor myself and keep my promise to myself. It has become less awkward as time has passed.

I don't ingest alcohol to alter my state to forget anymore, forcing me to deal with things I never wanted to look at before. I simply had to find a way to stop forgetting, stop burying before it buried me in the ground literally.

I am not perfect, and I have more work to do, but I am sober.

Charlotte Teggin

6

At 35, I finally cut my umbilical cord
HOW I GAVE REBIRTH TO MYSELF THROUGH FINDING MY VOICE

"The voice is the muscle of the soul."
Alfred Wolfsohn

I want to share my experience with you in the hope that it will help you or someone reading it learn about various ways of healing when dealing with grief and help you realize how grief can take you by surprise in a bad way. Maybe you don't need to fall into every pit I did. Being in a grieving state makes you react so weirdly in certain situations, and I, myself, did not see it coming. But life is such; it appears in small fractures, as we live it, moment by moment, and we can't see the larger picture till afterward. Maybe that is one way our body and mind save us and gets us through difficult times. So we can survive. My biggest survival tool has been my voice.

I am Thorey Sigthorsdottir, and in short, you could say I am a Renaissance woman. I am a free-lance working performance artist that has many hats for different roles. For me, they all connect; it is all about the soul of the human being, the magic of transformation, and creative communication. I am an actress, director, and voice, acting, and drama teacher.

I also work as a tour guide in the summer, which is perfect since I love to meet new and interesting people. I love to talk about my country, culture and I love to travel.

I was born in Iceland, raised in a small fishing village, Patreksfjördur, in the beautiful Westfjords. When I was eleven, I moved to Reykjavik, the capital, where I live now.

I have two children, my daughter Hera, who I gave birth to on my Christmas vacation in my second year at drama school. Ten days later, I was back in school doing the Greeks, hence her name :) Of course, she has now become an actress and is working internationally; Hera Hilmar.

Thirteen years passed until I had my second child, a son, Oddur Sigthor. I had planned my pregnancy with my first child. I thought it was quite practical to have her during school so I could focus on my carrier after graduation. Suddenly thirteen years had passed, and my son just made it to us before we stopped thinking about having children. "The same father?" you might be thinking. Yes, indeed. My son Oddur has been studying for the last semester in Folkehøjskole (Folk High School) in Denmark, preparing to become a film director, like his father. So the apple and the oak once again.

I divorced my husband Hilmar in 2010, and today I have a new partner, Jakob. We found each other just after I biked The Jakob's Road, the pilgrimage journey from Sevilla to Santiago de Compostela, Spain. "The Way." A funny coincidence!

I love to inspire and transform people, either through the art of performance or through helping them find their voice. Finding my voice has been one of the most spectacular healing journeys, and this is why I want to share my story with you.

Apocalyptic aftermath of birth

I am taking a shower, trying to decide if I will accept many liters of blood into my body; when washing, I find a lump in my breast. I can feel the cold sweat bursting out in the hot shower. Can it be true? A lump? Do I have cancer? I finish the shower, and I can feel the anxiety creeping into my soul.

It was the 7th of September 2001, and I had just given birth to my second child, a baby boy. My firstborn, my daughter, was 12 going on 13. The pregnancy had gone perfectly well. But as with my daughter, the boy was taking his time to come into the world. Both went 12 days over the expected time. Finally, I was in labor. With my daughter, we were at the hospital early, as soon as I felt the contractions, to be on the safe side. In the end, it was about 24 hours until the birth, with the labor slowly getting harder. We were prepared, playing classical music we had carefully selected, and some afro music to play when it would be time. In the end, the birth took over, and we both forgot everything about music until our beautiful daughter was born, healthy with a little cone head since a little help was needed from the suction clock.

Sex bomb

This time, thirteen years later, I was older and more experienced, so I wanted to take things into my hands. I was inspired by a wonderful book I had come across. It was focused on a natural birth method. There was a lot about using gravity. What also stood out for me was the method of opening the mouth and jaw to help the baby's head come out and to use the voice, easing the pain of the contraction.

No worries, I was ready with my sounds and was amazed when I found it working. What power I could feel, using my voice and not giving a fuck if everyone in the hospital could hear me.

There is no classical music this time, but instead dancing to Tom Jones' "Sex bomb.. you're my sex bomb," using the gravity and making my sounds in the contractions.

Is he alive?

This birth was the same process as with my firstborn, but now I knew what I was doing. I knew my body, and I was in control. It was all well until the *lightmother* (this was chosen as the most beautiful word in the Icelandic and means midwife) called the doctor for extra help at the most crucial moment. The baby's head was coming out, but suddenly there was deadly silence. I gave a worried look to the *lightmother*, who looked back at me as if to assure me: "Everything is fine," but I could feel the tension in the air.

Suddenly the doctor grabbed the baby, turned it upside down, and finally, he cried out. He was alive. I could feel the tears of joy and feeling of relief stream through my body. I did it, still in my little, black dress. All covered in blood.

You are not going anywhere.

I was preparing to leave the hospital with my husband and my newborn boy the next day when the nurse casually said: "Oh, but first we need to check your blood." "No problem," I thought, that made sense to me as a standard procedure. But when seeing the results, she looked at me, "You are not going anywhere." The numbers were way under what was normal.

So my son and I were moved to the maternity department. That is quite a depressing place to visit with your newborn baby since that is where all the mothers stay that are having difficulties with their pregnancies. It was a good reminder of how lucky I was, having been able to give birth to a healthy child.

I recall when I was pregnant with my daughter; being a young mother, my doctor emphasized the necessity to take iron, and I obeyed, of course. Which came in handy since I did lose a lot of blood when I gave birth to her, but I just managed.

This time around, I was very aware of eating healthy, and I didn't think I needed any extra iron, so I left it out. So when again I did lose a lot of blood, now I had run out of resources.

When you lose so much blood, the doctors are not allowed to give you blood unless your life depends on it. They need you to give an informed agreement before receiving it. I, who as a young woman often went to give blood to the blood bank, had never felt strange about giving or receiving blood. This time though, the idea of being injected by someone else's blood suddenly felt like an abhorrent idea. Somebody's else's life and blood in my veins? The thought was completely repellent to me, like having an alien at home.

Mother knows best

I thought I would need to discuss this with my mother, a practicing paramedic, to help me make this decision that suddenly sounded too challenging for me. My mother has always been my spiritual guide. She was the healer for other people, although she wasn't always there for herself.

The doctors said that if I decided to get blood immediately, about 4-8 liters, I would be able to go home the next day and take care of my baby without a problem. On the other hand, if I would decide to eat my way to better blood, saying no to the injections, I would need to have someone constantly around for the next months to help me with the baby. I would not be able to be alone with him

This sounded like an easy choice, but I needed to take my time to digest the idea of somebody else's blood running in my veins. Who knew what that blood had been through. That is when I went to take a shower and found a lump in my breast. What?! Now I have discovered I have cancer, or what!? After the shower, I just about managed to build up the courage to breathe this out and let go of the idea when confiding in my *lightmother*. She tried to comfort me, said that it was quite common to find a lump when you have just given birth, and usually, it turns out to be a stifled mammary gland. Which it was.

I returned to my baby, where he was lying "tanning" with "sunglasses" because of the newborn jaundice he had. He seemed very relaxed and feeling good, so I tried my best not to think about the foreign blood entering my body or possible cancer.

Suddenly my husband calls me from the drama school where he was teaching: "Have you heard the news?" with an apocalyptic sound in his voice, and my immediate response was: "No, and don't tell me." This was the day we never forget.

This was 9/11, 2001

My bed at the hospital happened to be in the room just opposite the TV room. Everybody gathered to look at the television streaming live images from NYC, with the airplanes flying into the World Trade Centre building.

I had just given birth to a child into a world that was collapsing. Nobody knew what was going to happen, if World War III had just started, or what? I only knew I didn't want to hear any of this. I needed to protect myself and be there for my baby. I needed all my strength to take care of my child.

This, too, did pass

The world kept turning, and this too did pass. I decided to accept the blood that I was offered. I could relax with the idea after talking to my cousin, who had had the same experience and survived. It is so weird how you change mentally and emotionally and become vulnerable when your body becomes feeble. The reason for my anxiety was the same; it was caused by; my lack of blood. I felt as fragile as a feather but quickly gathered my strength after receiving many liters of blood. The boy and I eventually got out of the hospital and went back home, where my husband and our wonderful daughter were waiting with her two excited grandmothers. All of them eager to get to know this little boy better and make him feel all the love that was there waiting for him.

Confirmation

Easter is coming up, and the 1st of April is going to be a big day in the family. Our daughter, Hera, is going to be confirmed. My husband and I are planning the confirmation party with Hera, and my mother, Sólrún, as usual, takes an active part. The confirmation day is wonderful, and I am surprised by the deep feeling I felt as a mother, looking at my daughter in the church. This felt so grown up. My little daughter was becoming a young woman. In the celebrations afterward, she welcomed the guests with a charming speech and played the cello, and then both of her grandmothers gave beautiful, heartwarming speeches. Both of them, my mother Sólrún and Hilmar's mother Borghildur, had been very involved with Hera's upbringing.

We had never needed a babysitter, even if I had to work a lot in the evenings in the theatre or teaching; they were always there, ready to come and help us out.

The moment when everything changed

Ten days later, on a Saturday, my husband and I are asleep in our bed with the cradle beside us when we hear the doorbell ring. We both wake up and look at the clock, then at each other, with the look of: "Someone ringing the doorbell this early on a Saturday is not good news." Then Hera comes into the room and says: "The priest is here, and a man with her." Immediately I thought: "Car accident! My mother." She was working outside of town and could have been in an accident during the morning rush hour, going to her morning shift.

The animal instinct

My movements have never been so heavy as when dressing this morning. In the silence, I could feel my husband, and I were both thinking the same. We left the room and knew things would never be the same.

Since I am an actress, I have often wondered about people's reactions in extreme situations like this, but this experience was completely surreal. As soon as the priest opens her mouth to announce the death of my mother, I could feel the scream leaving my body... No No No...and my body storming around the apartment. The animal instinct took over. At that moment, I didn't think of my 13-year-old daughter witnessing me, herself losing her grandmother that she was so close to. My husband calmed me down, and I embraced my daughter, and this unforeseen journey of my grief began.

The last moment we had together

My mother had been babysitting the night before while Hilmar and I went to a concert. We came home, found her asleep on the sofa. I can still picture her a bit confused waking up when we arrived. I remember her hugging me at the door, waving goodbye with a smile, and off she went in her car, home as it turned out, where she died later that night. The next day she didn't turn up for work, and eventually, they sent the police to check and see if she was alright. She was found at the kitchen table as if she had fallen asleep. We didn't find out until the day after.

Without a warning

There was no preparation, nothing that had been indicating that she was sick. Afterward, we did see, when looking at the photos from the confirmation and more, that she hadn't been looking so healthy, and her sister, Dagný Björk, said she had been complaining about some pain in her back. My mother did tend to have high blood pressure, but she was not too keen on going to the doctors herself since she worked in the hospital. She knew too much about what they could find out, I guess. It turned out to be coronary occlusion that killed her, and the doctors said it would not have changed anything if someone would have been with her. She could not have been saved, and that was a bit of a relief in some weird way.

A transformation I didn't ask for

Before this, I had never been the super-anxious-type-of-a-person. After my mother's death, and possibly because of my already vulnerable state, being a newborn mother, my nervous system was invaded in a very harsh way.

I am sharing this story with you because looking back now, almost 20 years later, I can see so many things that could have been dealt with better. That being said, it leads me to a journey of many various healing methods in the attempt to try to live with my grief and stay sane for my children. In the end, the most important tool for my survival was my work with the voice. I will go more into that later. It kept me connected to my core, while life took me into many different directions during this period of pain where I felt like I was losing myself.

What I learned was to live with my sorrow, and I can say now, truthfully, I would not have wanted to miss the journey my grief led me into since through that, I have learned so much about myself on a deeper level I could ever imagine.

The dream project

In 2000, the Millennium and my husband Hilmar Oddsson were working on our dream project, a multi-media performance of Medea by Euripides, with our theatre group. I am producing, I wrote the adaptation of the play with Inga Lísa Middleton, a filmmaker, and a close friend, and Hilmar is directing. We receive a big production grant from the European Commission - Culture 2000, meaning we will premiere in Reykjavik and then tour England and Finland with our performance.

The fertility of creative power

Ironically, working on Medea, a play about a mother who kills her children in the attempt to get revenge on her husband, I became pregnant with my second child (and by the director!). Consequently, we were forced to apply for a delay of the tour till summer 2002. It was too much of an absurd idea and did not serve the performance; to have Medea heavily pregnant.

Touring in Europe in the aftermath of 9/11

Here I was, in 2002, still in a shock after my mother's death, but I had to fulfill the contract with the European Commission and carry on with our planned tour to England and Finland. When asking for the delay, little did we know how different our lives would be only a year later?

The performances went well, and the tour was a success, but every flight was torture. I had to drink two to three glasses of Gin and Tonic before going on board to comfort my fear. Whenever I saw someone who looked Arab to me, my heart started to beat faster, imagining the worst. I was aware of my mental state and my prejudices, being super sensitive with a very vivid imagination. Still heavily in my grief and agitated by the events of 9/11.

A safe space to grief.

One of my natural defense mechanisms in life is to keep myself busy. That is, in a way, also where I find my worthiness. It is how I got praised as a child, by being an achiever; a doer. In March 2003, I was close to emotional exhaustion. The touring had been demanding, I had written the report to the European Commission, which was a huge task, and Christmas had been difficult, being the first Christmas after my mother died.

So, I immediately jumped on the wagon when a good friend told me about a silent retreat held at Skálholt, an old bishopric and a cultural center in the south of Iceland. This very retreat was organized by the women working in the Lutheran Church (state religion of Iceland), and it was exactly what I needed at that moment. A safe space to allow me to grief. Since my mother's death, the time had been so busy and demanding for me with all my projects.

When going to Skálholt, I got a lift with one of the ladies attending the retreat, and when she arrived at my house in her tiny little car, in the middle of the winter, icy roads, I got a shock. The cold sweat appeared again. I had to take a few deep breaths before joining her and was very grateful when she (the first time I saw someone do this) did a little prayer, surrounding the car with angel armor and blessed it for the road. I joined her in my mind because I was sure this wouldn't be safe. This habit I actually picked up and still do all the time when traveling.

Women with big hearts and strong faith.

I was in Skálholt for five days with these wonderful women that I had never met before. Some of them were priests, some working with the 12 steps program, and some had been missionaries in Africa. Women with big hearts and strong faith. In this environment, I experienced for the first time the magic of spending time in silence with others in a program, and it was powerful and trans-formative.

The first night when we were introducing ourselves, I could hardly speak. I had this big lump in my throat, and when I, the last one to be introduced, tried to explain why I had decided to join, only a few words managed to make their way out. Every one of these women reminded me of my mother, with their warm smiles and a hearty presence. We spoke the first night, but then we went into complete silence, executing our daily tasks in silence. One rule intro-duced was that every time we met someone at the table having meals or walking in the corridors, we were to mentally send each other good thoughts.

This was so unique, being in the space with someone and not having to say a word. Exactly what I needed. I was just sending and receiving good thoughts. All the ceremonies and prayers that we could choose to participate in or not were also really helpful in the grieving process.

Facing myself in solitude

There was plenty of time to write down one's thoughts. I was so angry at my mother for not taking good care of herself or going to regular checks with her doctor. That became very clear to me; I had to find a way to forgive her somehow. The prayers and the community of women were a great help. I took this very seriously, practicing the silence, except when I sneaked off to my room to call my husband. My son had a fever when I left home, so I had almost decided not to go, but my husband encouraged me to stick to my plan. He would take care of things at home, and I was grateful for that. But of course, my thoughts were also with the boy, so I had to check in and see how he was doing.

This silent retreat was very important for me in dealing with my sorrow and gave me the strength to carry on. This was my first silent retreat, but not my last, and I recommend this to anyone going through a challenging time in their life. I do have to say; it is indeed a challenge to look yourself in the eyes and see what is really going on in you, as this forced me to do when being alone with myself and my thoughts. So be prepared. Although I wasn't, actually, prepared. I just took the leap of faith.

Bad omens in superstition get a life of their own.

My healing did not happen overnight. I had to grab my thoughts again and again and turn them the right way. If I saw a raven, or not to mention many together, the cold sweat appeared. Bad omen! I read into all superstition that happened. I imagined the worst, and then I had to wind down my thoughts and get my heart to beat slower.

For many years any kind of traveling became a challenge for me. Immediately, when putting down dates for a trip for the family or work, I would look at the date and read into the numbers looking for a sign of bad luck. Whenever we had to change dates, I would feel the cold sweat again and my heart beating, but I didn't talk to anyone about this. I was sure it would make things worse, actually make it a reality.

Fear makes you act in strange ways.

Like our planned trip to Cuba, my husband and I always wanted to visit Cuba. When he raised the possibility, I agreed with my heart thumping in my chest, and we started to plan. We even bought the tickets, but all the time we were planning the trip, deciding on the dates and all, I would break out in cold sweats. So finally, when Hilmar started to have doubts as well because of financial reasons, I agreed. We should skip it, and we did.

Many years later, when I was going through my stuff after our divorce, I came across the old receipt for the trip. I looked at it and started crying. It all came back to me; it was all still in my body, this energy of anxiety.

The time is now.

We decided to get married on summer solstice 2003, just over a year after my mother's death. One of the responses to her death was to finally do it. We had been planning to get married for years but never agreed on the time and place and the execution of it. We had even made the guest list with my mother on top. Death in the family makes you think about the virtue of time. Don't wait for the right time to do things. The time is now.

We got married in the Reykjavik Cathedral 21st of June 2003. It was a beautiful moment, and our children participated in the ceremony. Of course I was crying, tears of joy and grieving that guest of honor number one, my mother, and that she wasn't there to celebrate with us.

The precious moments.

We went to Spain with the children on a honeymoon. On one of our first days there, we visited Sevilla, a beautiful city in close vicinity. It was very hot, and we forgot the baby carriage in the house. This caused a lot of stress, so we decided Hilmar would drive back to get it, and I would wait with the children.

An hour later, when he came back, we explored this beautiful city and enjoyed the trip—filming it all on our video camera.

An unforeseen accident.

Two days later, exchanging the tape in the video camera for a new one, we realized that Hilmar had, in the stress in Sevilla, accidentally recorded over the wedding tape. What we had left were just a few minutes, where we were seen leaving the altar after the ceremony.

I completely lost it. Somehow inside, I felt this was a really bad omen for our relationship and the marriage. Also, I felt that my husband showed a lack of respect for our relationship since he didn't take better care of the valued recording of our wedding in the first place.

All my insecurity blew up, making this whole thing a disaster. Eventually, I calmed down, but I had difficulties forgiving him for a while. All my reactions were entirely out of proportion.

My toolbox my savior.

Time passed, and I was going to all kinds of healers to help me make it through this overall grief I was still experiencing. I also realized I was ever so lucky to have the tools I originally got to work on myself as an actor. The most powerful healing tool, if any, I have discovered on myself is the voice.

I had gotten to know the voice work of an amazing woman, Nadine George, in 1996, and from 1999 I regularly went to her international workshops in London. Later on, I became an accredited teacher of the NG Voice Work.

Nadine is a wonderful teacher that creates the most trusting and creative space for her actors to work in. Originally, part of this work came from a man, Alfred Wolfsohn. He had healed himself from the trauma of being at war, in WW1, through his work with the sounds of his voice. Roy Hart later learned from him and adapted Wolfsohn's work into theatre, forming his own theatre group, which Nadine became a part of. After Roy Hart died, she left the theatre group and adapted her own structure of the voice work, Nadine George Voice Work.

That is another story I will not go into here, but Nadine's voice work became my tightrope through my sorrow. It is a very creative tool for an actor, but it is also very healing for anyone on a very deep level.

By mixing Nadine's work with meditation in movement, like Chi Gong exercises, I released tons of tears, which kept me sane, if anything did. Enough at least to carry on. I still wasn't back to my normal self. That took many years, and of course, my normal self will never be the same.

Four years had passed.

My husband wrote a song for me when I turned 40, and at the birthday party, he sang it to me with the lyrics: "Thorey - birthday child...," a kind of sing-along text that later he wrote proper lyrics too. The song's name became *"Angel,"* and in the song, he was singing to his angel (me), and I again burst out in a cold sweat. I was in shock. I could hardly listen to the song because I found it so morbid; it had to indicate something, this angel talk. Yet, I didn't say anything to him about how I felt about it.

What does the voice work mean?

But I kept on going, doing my voice work. I always went back to that when I felt I was going to a bad place in myself.

To help you understand better the elements of what I am talking about, working with the voice means a lot of breathwork, connection to your core essence, connecting the voice and the body, releasing tension from the body, releasing mental blocks and old beliefs that hinder you; so this goes extremely well in hand with someone who is dealing with emotional trauma.

Especially the NG Voice Work since it includes a lot of active breathwork and works with the sounds of our voice in such a creative and healing way. Where you allow the voice to be all it is, with its ugliness and demons, we so often try to cover up with our behavior.

"I lost my mother eight years ago..." well... Is this still the real reason for my suffering?

A turning point. I finally did go to see my doctor and talked to him about my feelings and state of mind, my anxiety. He told me I was entitled to apply for group therapy at the mental department of the National Hospital, in Cognitive Behavioural Therapy or CBT. I was lucky. I hadn't heard about this possibility before. Usually, it was quite expensive to get this therapy, but it was way cheaper through my doctor. Since there was some time until I would be able to join. Since there was some time until I would be able to join. I got sessions with a psychiatrist, for one-fourth of the usual price, to help me prepare for the group program

When the psychiatrist started interviewing me about my reasons for joining the program, I started my *"8 years ago I lost my mother very suddenly"*... mantra only to realize this time it felt and sounded so unreal. Was there maybe something else broken?

Finally, in these sessions with the psychiatrist, I unraveled the broken situation at home. I realized there was tension between me and my husband that was now causing a lot of my stress and anxiety. This, in short, lead to my divorce in the same year, 2010.

Writing my story, all these years later, I realize how my life started to deteriorate after the loss of my mother. My whole nervous system broke down, eventually making all my traumas rise to the surface where I could see them, feel them and take action. All my old wounds were startled. Somehow my husband was not in alignment with my process. He had his own shadows to face. One probably being depression that he had not dealt with, leading to many explosions of anger in our communication, which again lead to us drifting further and further away from each other. Unable to communicate our feelings and find our way to strengthen our relationship. Then it was too late.

I will not go further into the divorce process, but in the end, we are still good friends, and I am grateful for that. I will always love him for being the father of my children and for our lives together.

The onion of healing and transformation.

It has been eleven years since my divorce. Eleven years of personal transformation. I feel that trauma of this kind that I went through can stir up deeper wounds. At least in my case. I became like an onion. I was working on myself, dealing with my grief. I have gone through layers of wounds belonging to my life since my childhood and possibly from previous lives. I met psychiatrists and healers of all sorts that helped me in my process, eventually leading to me in 2018 participating in an Ayahuasca cere- mony. (*Ayahuasca is a South American psychoactive brew used both socially and as a ceremonial, spiritual medicine among the indigenous peoples of the Amazon basin*)

That experience was like the voice work, or the energy work, amplified ten times, and I felt a lot of release and healing through and after that powerful ceremony. I was in the safe and loving hands of a very experienced Shaman from Peru who knew exactly what he was doing, and I would never go into this ceremony without making sure I was in good hands.

A new opening.

That same year I was invited by Jóhanna Jónasdóttir, an Icelandic actress and a very powerful healer of the Barbara Brennan practice herself, to an event with a native American Shaman. Her name is Patricia Whitebuffalo, and together we worked through dance and the voice. I loved it.

When Patricia announced she would be offering a three-year study in shamanic healing in Iceland, I decided to join. This came as such a logical step after all my energy work and search through the voice.

The way home.

I am now in the middle of my shamanic healing study, just about to finish the second year. It has been such a powerful transformation, and finally, I feel like I am coming home to myself. Awakening to my real self and connecting to my core essence. All the pieces of the puzzles are finally coming together, although I think for me, the transformative way of living is a never-ending story. You can always go deeper. As with the voice.

For me, the element of finding my voice has happened on a much deeper level than just being able to make my sound resonate and being able to transform myself into a role as an actor but finding my true essence in the voice connected to my soul and allowing that to happen.

My voice is with me at all times, and I use it as my personal healing tool. This helps me connect all the experiences I had with my various healers and process them through my body.

My biggest lesson.

I know in some way I was pushed into this journey through the death of my mother. So in a weird way, my mother, who was the one who introduced me to spiritual matters in the first place and awoke my interest in both theatre and personal development, was the one who brought me through to the next level. For that, I am grateful.

I hope to become a role model for my children in how they deal with their lives, in their ups and downs in this roller-coaster life can be for us human beings. We are so small in the big cosmos, yet still, we are so big if we allow ourselves to stay in the light, being true to the people we really are, in alignment with our highest purpose.

When you hit rock bottom, the only way out is up.

In the year 2018, I hit rock bottom emotionally. I had gone through a couple of very challenging relationships with men, and the experiences that pulled me down but were a huge and valuable lesson in the end.

When it comes to it, it is always your own decision where you put your boundaries in a relationship, and I was getting my biggest lesson now.

I participated in a very cathartic performance that leads me to open an old wound of sexual abuse I had experienced as a teenager and buried deep down inside. Still, now there was time to face that trauma. So I took talking sessions to help me deal with the consequences of that experience.

Letting go

I also finally decided to sell my big apartment, which I had kept after my divorce, and that was not an easy decision to make. That apartment was so loaded with my family dreams with my husband, and I felt I really needed to let go of it to be able to move forward emotionally in my relationships.

So, the summer of 2018 was a bit of horror for me. I have to admit that I actually experienced for the first time in my life that maybe I might as well give up and walk into the ocean.

Just for a brief moment. I was ready to give up; I felt it was all hopeless, and nobody would care if I left.

The light at the end of the tunnel.

I see it now as the big darkness before it gets bright—the final bottom before I kicked myself up into the light. In the summer, my hands were full, moving out of my house, clearing it, going through all the stuff that comes along with two apartments. I had been renting it out to students and was living in another house. So I had two apartments to empty with all the stuff. Then I was forced to move to my uncle's apartment until I would get my new apartment since my landlord was not ready to give me any extra time there. At the same time, I was tour-guiding a lot to support myself, giving my smile and energy to people. It was madness. I was pushing myself to my limits.

My pilgrimage to Santiago De Compostela.

After the moving I came across an ad for a biking tour in September, cycling from Sevilla to Santiago De Compostela, in Spain "The Camino," a two-week tour on a mountain bike. I signed up for it. The Jacob's road, as it is called, little did I know what that would lead to. This was my pilgrimage, clearing my mind after this big transition I was going through in my life.

It was a wonderful group I traveled with, and our guide was excellent. I cried my way biking through Spain...(easy on a bike since no one noticed), and in the evenings, we were like little kids laughing away in ecstasy after the physical exercise and all the oxygen.

Wow, I was ever so grateful to make it to Santiago De Compostela, where our journey ended. Everyone in one piece. I was moved to tears at the Cathedral when our names were read out at the ceremony, and it warmed my heart receiving the pilgrimage certification. It truly was a pilgrimage for me on a deep level. I left so many things that were not serving me anymore on "The Camino" for good.

New beginning

I came back to Iceland, and within a week, I met... my Jakob! A beautiful, loving man who I can laugh with and who is the same lover of nature and traveling. I am in love. I carry on with my theatre-making, my shamanic healing study, and my teachings, full of gratitude for the people in my life; the presents my experience has given me.

The journey continues.

In 2019 on Easter, I was inspired by a good friend Magga went hiking in Peru to Machu Picchu, a place of beauty and high spiritual energy. I just made the last trip they did with The Icelandic Mountain Guides before covid-19 stopped all traveling.

During the covid-19 times, there have been many new lessons in resilience and realizing the power of online teaching and learning. Even with my shamanic healing.

I have returned home to my heart, and my love for life and myself have never been as deep, in the most genuine and generous way.

Hold the space for your loved ones

Speak your truth

Listen, your voice is your road going home

I am home wherever I am.

Home is my heart.

Home is me.

Home.

Reykjavik 4th July 2021
Thorey Sigthorsdottir

7

Flame Thrower

MY DIVINE SPARK IS STRONGER THAN ANY
DARK DRAGON.

**"Don't ever accept anyone else's preconceived
limitations. If there's something you want to do. There
isn't any reason you can't do it."**
Amy Dodson

I finally achieved my goal despite him and his
hypocritical rhetoric. I crushed my goal! I am not his
mother and never will be. His mom, Mary, is a home-
maker who has never worked outside the home. She is a
first-generation Italian who stays home drinking pots of
coffee, smoking cigarettes, watching soap operas, cooking,
and raising her last three of seven kids. She only left the
house for Mass and to get her hair done every Thursday. A
wonderful lady and accepting of me dating her favorite
son! Although she wouldn't come to our wedding because
it wasn't in a Catholic Church. We were married outside

under the stars with friends and family. I called her the spaghetti Mama and that fate was not for me. I had to get out and do whatever was necessary.

Well, though I wasn't raised by a military family; I had a military idea. Telling me that I can't go to the police academy now that I am a mother is pure bullshit. I supported my husband during his nine months of off-campus police academy training. He was to graduate on June 04, 1989. Tim worked as a contractor building houses, then went to the academy Monday through Thursday evenings and all day on Saturday. This schedule left him only Sundays with his family.

I was a single parent during these times. I would read his law books to get a head start and couldn't wait to start the academy. My days consisted of starting the generator to get power for lights, and the generator pumped the well water into our home. The refrigerator and stove ran on propane. We had purchased this two-story, three-bedroom with two bathrooms the previous year in 1988 in Auburn, California. Our first home on 14 acres was where I could have my horses, goats, chickens, sheep, and a vegetable garden. We had been renting the previous years after our marriage on September 25, 1984. Then I would get the babies breakfast, feed the animals, and get ready for work. I was waitressing at the Auburn Valley Country Club. Tim did not like that one bit. He despised sharing me with anyone and especially did not want me working out of the house. He was very jealous of any man that would look at me and would become confrontational. Looking back all those years ago, I see now that I married a narcissist.

I had wanted to be many things growing up in the 60's and 70's, a horse trainer, flight stewardess, join the US Air Force to be a helicopter pilot, join Dian Fossey's soldiers protecting her and her gorilla group in Africa. Boy, oh boy, did I lose my shit when I read that on December 26, 1985, Dian Fossey was hacked to death with a machete. I wanted to be a radio DJ, a model, join a band. So many interests that I blame on my Attention Deficit Disorder-ADHD, Obsessive-Compulsive Disorder-OCD, and Complex Post Traumatic Stress Disorder-CPTSD that I do not want to try out just one occupation in this lifetime. I wanted to learn so many things. When it came to law enforcement, I was passionate about becoming a police officer. And, I had my reasons.

I left Tim on the day he graduated from the academy. I attended the ceremony with the kids. I would not put up with his infidelity one more time. It was the same modus operandi every time he screwed around on me. Always a young girl 16 or 17 years old that he seduced at their work. The first affair, if you will, that I caught him in was with a blond girl that worked at the boat repair shop named Trina. Back in the late '80s, we did not have mobile phones, but we did have pagers. One day Tim left his pager when he went to work. After you called the pager number, you put it up to the phone, then pushed the button and it emanated a tone that retrieved the voice mailbox. I checked his messages and heard a girl's voice.

Trina said to meet her at the liquor store parking lot for some vodka and a quicky. I went numb, shaking while trying to process what I had just heard. Where the hell does he get time to work, go to the academy, and fuck around? I showed up and confronted them, screaming like a banshee straight out of the Irish countryside moors. Of course, Tim denied that he was messing around and to get my ass home now. I went to a friend's house with our baby girl for a few days until Tim gaslighted me enough to believe he was innocent, and I went back home. This happened four times in two years. The final straw was when I discovered he was screwing my baby sister Katrina. I place the blame 80% on Tim and 20% on Katrina. She must've gotten this trait from our momma because I was far from interested in sex. I was so frightened of the male body and completely frigid. She was born when I was 11, and I raised her as my own because our mom was busy with work, dating, divorcing, and getting married. Katrina's crib was put in my bedroom with my sister, and we tended to her thorough the night. When she was older, we joked that she was my firstborn!

One of the saddest parts of his infidelity is that I blamed myself for his running around because of my female issues and surgeries. These began when I was 19, and I had a different diagnosis each time I saw a new doctor. After three laparoscopies (exploratory surgeries via the belly button), it was determined that I had Pelvic Inflammatory Disease (an infection of a woman's reproductive organs. This is generally caused by sexually transmitted diseases) and Cervical Dysplasia (abnormal growth of cells on the surface of the cervix considered a precancerous condition). It took me a year and a half to conceive my baby girl Jessica, who was born by emergency cesarean section after her heart stopped on the monitor. Tim used to joke that he married me for my great teeth and big hips, just like when you pick out a great broodmare! Tim and I were in the birthing room at Auburn Faith Hospital on January 17, 1986. We were using the LaMaze Method breathing technique we had trained for at the hospital's program. It would teach me to focus through the labor pains to have a natural, unmedicated delivery. Tim even did the extra class to permit him in the surgery room if the delivery became an emergency. When her heart stopped, the delivery nurse went to the wall to push a button, flipped on the overhead lights, and told me to turn over and get on all fours, doggie style.

Mind you. I am wearing a hospital gown that is spilt open all down the back. When I get on all fours, my whole body is exposed, minus my neck, where it is tied, and my arms. In the room rushed two more nurses who are manipulating my baby bump to turn the baby. Still no heartbeat. Tim is trying to get answers to what is happening while I am using the breathing technique from our Lamaze class, "he he he-ing and who who who-ing," breathing to stay focused. I begin making deals with God and Goddess, Angels and Ancestors to save my baby while all the commotion around me had me scared that I was losing this baby. Next thing you know, one of the nurses tells Tim to come with her to get scrubbed for surgery. The wheels on my bed are unlocked, and away we go racing down the hall to the surgery room with me on my hands and knees, ass out and forward, riding backward. I was knocked out pretty quickly after Tim arrived in hospital scrubs, a mask, and a hat.

After surgery, I woke up in the maternity room with Tim sitting next to me, holding my hand. He said our daughter had wrapped the umbilical cord around her neck and nearly died. She was in the oxygen tent and would be brought to me in an hour. Jessica Ann was the most beautiful creature I ever laid eyes on.

Our son, my miracle baby, was born 18 months later with a cleft lip. I had a 10% chance of conception and was using a diaphragm. He was going to have surgery at four months old to repair his lip and nose. Tim couldn't deal with the very idea of a defective son.

Tim had taken a job with a bank to build homes two hours from our home. They put him up in an apartment there, and he would come home on weekends. I would check his pager, as he had girlfriends over in Fairbanks. He didn't come home for my birthday. He said he was too overwhelmed with work and had to catch up.

One day I was able to view the video my friend Kitty made of our son's birth. I see Tim coming out of the delivery room saying, "there's no way that's my kid." That broke my heart that Tim would say that. After my four-month-old's surgery, I made a sling and carried the baby around, force-feeding him through a feeding tube syringe because his surgeon said he shouldn't nurse for it might tear the tiny sutures. I cried for weeks while I cuddled my baby, who desperately wanted to nurse, and I so wanted him to!

My children and I moved to a friend's duplex across the street from the high school and left the ranch. I put the cheque box and credit cards on the kitchen table. I only packed some clothes and toys and a few kitchen items. When I returned to the ranch to gather more of our things, I found a note taped to the doors and windows that stated, "DO NOT ENTER OR SUFFER BODILY HARM." What in the actual f**k? Tim did not want me to retrieve anything from our home?

Yeah, NO! I took a rock and broke the back door window, and reached down to unlock the door. Ouch! When I looked in, I found he had taped razor blades to the lock and knob. I grabbed a baby blanket from my Bronco and pushed the blades off the lock, and gained entry. My friend Becky and I packed up some household items, baby furniture, and a few odds and ends and left.

Three days later, I received a collect call from the Placer County Jail; it was Tim. It turned out a neighbor was checking on the ranch and called the cops because he thought the house was broken into and robbed. When the sheriff deputies arrived, they called the Bomb Squad based on the threatening notes posted. So here's Tim, a law enforcement academy graduate the previous month currently interviewing with agencies to get hired, and he's in jail! Oh, the irony is just too much. Hell NO, I will not bail your twisted ass out!

I am a big U2 fan and went to their Joshua Tree concert in November 1997. It was raining in San Francisco the night of the concert, and Tim refused to go. I said I was going to pick up his brother's wife to go to the concert. Her husband Jimmy said she wasn't going anywhere! I told her to run outside, and I would pick her up, and we would go to the concert in San Francisco. We drove to San Francisco in the pouring rain and even picked up two hitchhikers. They were broken down and had a sign saying U2 or bust. We made it to the show just as the sky broke open and the sun shone down. We had a phenomenal time at our first U2 concert!

Sometime later, I went to the cinema with Becky to see U2's new movie "Rattle and Hum". When we came out of the cinema, my Bronco was gone! I later found out that Tim had taken my truck. The following day after work, I went to pick up my kids at daycare only to be told that Tim had picked them up? At dinner time, I paged him to ask when he was bringing the kids home. There was no response. Several times a day, there was no response. After calling some of our mutual friends, I found out that he had moved in with a woman before he booby-trapped our house and had our babies at her house 30 minutes away. None of our so-called friends would tell me where she lived.

I knew this woman. She was the big sister of a friend of ours and a Placer County Sheriff's Deputy. So I called the Sheriff's office to speak with her Commanding Officer and filed a formal complaint that my kids were missing and in her home with my husband. I was told nothing could be done as we were not divorced, and there was no custody order in place. I complained to the Sheriff's office every day for 11 days until Tim finally called my home to say he was bringing the kids home. When he got my babies home, he wanted to talk. He said that he was in the final interviews for Davis Police Department and the next step was my character reference interview. My kids were returned as a ransom to lie to the investigator about his domestic violence arrest. I was to say that it was all my fault so he could get this job with DPD. I agreed—anything to get my baby's home.

Six months later, we were loading up after getting my Bronco back and hauling ass as far away from Tim as we could get. We landed in a beautiful beach town in Destin, Florida, on the Gulf of Mexico. Ahh, the healing crystal water and sugar-white beach sand.

At 32, I was accepted into the North Walton Community College Law Enforcement Training Center in Fort Walton Beach, Florida. Thirty-two years old, and I was the oldest cadet they ever accepted. I was a single mother of two. I was waitressing to make ends meet. I had also gotten my real estate license which was another big goal. It would be hard to juggle the kids, their school, my waitressing job with school four nights a week and every Saturday for nine months. But I was very determined, and when I set a goal, I crush it!

We lived in the bottom of a two-story duplex on the Western lake, near Destin, Florida, a stone's throw from the Gulf of Mexico. It was a beautiful and very healing home for us after leaving my husband in California. The kids were happy and healing. We went to the beach every day or paddled around on the little lake. We all made friends, and life was getting comfortable.

The college gave me resources to assist with my tuition, books, childcare, and scholarship resources for additional fees such as ammunition. It was a lot of legwork, but my determination far outweighed all the errands and red tape required.

My mom lived on the street in front of me with her fifth husband and did not support my police officer dream. She refused to help with the children, and we became very distanced. Not that we ever had a good relationship anyway. She never liked me because I look like my father, and she didn't want children so young when she had me at 16 years old. But that's another story.

I got Head Start through the county to send over a sitter, and my books were sorted when class began in April of 1994. Of the 28 cadets, there were four women. I was the oldest, and I felt like an outsider immediately. It's not unusual as I've been an outsider all my life. With my learning disability, I had to study every waking moment that I was not volunteering at the kid's school or coaching their softball games. Some of the classes were a breeze, but the law classes were quite tricky. I was not a quitter, so I pressed on.

Because of my good grades, I won a scholarship from Destin's Women's Center that paid for all of my ammunition, and they delivered it to the college. I've always been an excellent shooter and had such a great time shooting on the range. We were issued government 38 revolvers and shotguns. We all loaded our shotguns and aimed down-range. When I fired, the kickback was quite unexpected and threw me back a few feet. A flame shot out of the barrel about 3-4 feet long. Trainer Collings shouted for us to shoulder our weapons. He came to me to look at my ammo. The required ammo was birdshot, but the Women's Center had bought me high brass shells. The trainers and other cadets took turns shooting that ammo, and we all had a good time. I was given the nickname Flame Thrower!

Some of the macho men were jealous of my marksmanship and would say things like, "Murphy! Wait till we get in Defensive Tactics, combat!" The trainers found my grouping on my silhouette quite interesting when we'd walk downrange and look at our paper target silhouette, most other groupings were in the heart, but mine were in the groin. Trainer Collins, an officer with Pensacola PD, said, "Well, you certainly can tell Murphy's been divorced!" We all got a laugh out of that, and I finally made a friend with Denise, a fellow cadet. By this time, a female cadet had washed out, so there were just three girls left. We learned the history of firearms and how to take them apart to clean them. I was awarded Top Gun with a score of 100%!

Our physical training was at Eglin Air Force Base, where they had a fantastic obstacle course and trained Army Rangers. It was so thrilling. I did it better than the other two girls. We got to rappel from a three-story building, jump over hurdles, hang upside down on a rope with your leg tossed over, and shimmy across 25 ft! I got 100% on that course and felt more confident and gained some respect and atta-girl from my fellow cadets. We also had a partner assigned to us. My partner was a nice quiet guy called Sing Sing because his father was incarcerated in the

Sing Sing Correctional Facility in New York. Our nick-names were remarkably interesting.

One block we studied was public safety using tear gas, CN, and how to deploy on the public. We had to stand in the line and get spit on! And yelled at by the trainers right up in our faces. This taught us tolerance and how to buck up when we're in public and situations like this arise. We practice tackling each other safely, handcuffing, felony takedowns, and neck holds. It was very physical, and the two dudes that did not like me were very rough. But I never complained because I didn't want to look weak.

In June, our block course was defensive driving. The first part would be the classroom components about learning your vehicle and the special suspension installed in the squad cars. Then we would move out to the college parking lot to drive the cars! Fast! That first day was Friday, June 17, 1994, and as we filed into the classroom, the two trainers, who worked as deputy sheriffs, had the news on the TV, and we sat mesmerized as OJ took LAPD on a wild chase on the freeway! Many of the videos we watched in our training came from LAPD on what not to do and what good techniques to use. We all thought it was crazy that our first day learning how to drive a squad car correlated with the OJ chase!

I consider myself a pretty good music buff, having purchased my first album at 13 years old with my house cleaning money. It was The Bee Gees Sgt Pepper, and I still have it 45 years later! I've even been a DJ for a while. I have over 200 concert stubs and excel at music trivia. One day on the way to school, I called in to answer a trivia question on the radio. They played a 10-second clip of the song No Sugar Tonight. I heard a guy answer naming the band Bread, but he was wrong. I was next on the line to answer the Guess Who to win two tickets to see the band Traffic in Pensacola for their reunion tour! Steve Winwood and Jim Capaldi would be together again after breaking up in 1974. I could pick up the tickets at the station the following day for the show in Pensacola.

By this point, I was mentally and physically exhausted and went to the doctor, who wrote me a note for a few days off school to rest and hopefully make up the two missed days. It also correlated with the night of the Traffic concert that I took my friend James to, and it was extraordinary! I have been to many concerts to this one within the top 10, to be sure.

When we came out of the show, we saw two officers with flashlights shining on my Ford Taurus. Somebody had broken my driver's window and stole all my law enforcement manuals and books. When they wrapped up their crime scene, James and I headed back over to Destin. When we got into Fort Walton Beach, we were pulled over at gunpoint, also called a felony takedown. It turns out the officers thought I had stolen the car because of the broken window. I showed him my credentials for the training academy and my driver's license and insurance. When he called it in to dispatch, Brandy took the call. Brandy is the other female cadet in my class.

When I showed up at school the following Monday, I was called into the director's office. Mr. McFall was an imposing figure and an ex-FBI agent. He was a very stern and by-the-book kind of fellow. I'd been in his office too many times before. He said because he liked my grit, he wasn't going to dismiss me from the training center for attending a concert instead of school, but what he was going to do is make me repeat that course the following spring so I would not graduate with my class. I was heart-broken. And I could not decide if it was worth the cost to see Stevie Winwood with his old bandmates. My courses ended in November, and there was very little fanfare for me because I was still not finished, and I wasn't sure that I could go back the following spring.

Tim visited us for Christmas and brought me a Bad Boy's t-shirt from the reality cop show. He was supportive and looked over my books. Looking back, it's strange how we lived as a couple for those ten days. He and the kids and a few friends encouraged me to continue the course and take that last class. The following May, I took the final course, First Responder First Aid, that I was kicked out of. When I was coming out of class with all my fellow student cadets, I watched in horror as my Ford Taurus was hooked up to a tow truck and repossessed. The looks and sneers and whis-pers ostracized me yet again. During the last two weeks of class, I had friends drop me off, and I even hitchhiked several times to finish that course.

As I was hitchhiking home the last night, I was so happy that I had done everything to achieve my goal. But I was a little sad that I would not have a little graduation ceremony with my fellow cadets. I made it home at midnight to find the kids, and the babysitter had waited up for me. They had made a banner hanging in the kitchen that said Mom, you are my Hero with X's and O's! I was such a lucky mom because that was the best graduation party I could have ever had! We worked as a team, and we did it.

By this time, Tim convinced me to move to Colorado, where he would join me, and we could work things out to be a family again. He wanted me to fly the kids to him while I packed up and moved our things, and he would join me there. When I finally made it to Colorado Springs with my Chow Chow dog, China. I called him from a payphone only to hear him say he was not coming to Colorado after all. He had met a girl. Once I was stable... maybe the following summer.

This nearly destroyed me. What could I do? He said if I fought him or came back to claim the kids, he would have me arrested. He was a cop, and I did not have the finances to fight him. I camped in the forest until I picked up two jobs, bartending and commercial painting, to get a weekly motel. Then I saved money to hire an attorney. I enrolled in Pikes Peak Community College to cross-train in the three high liability courses, Defensive Driving, Defensive Tactics, and Firearms, to take the state exam to get my police officer certificate.

Once this was completed, I began applying at the various police departments in Colorado Springs and nearby towns. After three months, it became apparent that I was never going to get hired. With over 4,000 applicants and limited openings, I didn't stand a chance. I didn't have a degree, and that's what a lot of these departments were looking for.

Screw it. I had a better idea that would give me the freedom to make my own hours and choose my jobs. So, I walked into Bobby Brown Bail Bonds and asked for a job. He sent me to a weekend course for the average Joe to get a bounty hunting ID card. I excelled after all of my extensive training and began bounty hunting with my friend Tom who used to be a Delta Force army guy. I found jumpers on the FBI Most Wanted. We suited up, did our research, and reconnaissance to find these guys. I selected men who had a history of domestic violence. Men who had warrants for rape. Men who jumped bail with a history of child incest and/or molestation. We picked up horrible men who had hurt women and children. There were a few other jumpers like drug dealers that we picked up as well.

More than a few times, I could walk into a bar to arrest the guy. I am a tall, pretty redhead and did some modeling in LA in the late '70s. I would send a drink or a shot to the perpetrator to get his attention. The dudes would always come over to my table to talk with me. I would be flirtatious, and one thing would lead to another, and I moved in for the kill. This is when I would invite him back to my place and go to my truck. That is when Tom would present himself, and we showed our badge and arrested the guy. Then we took them to the closest police station and waited for our check in the mail from the Bail Bond Company.

Even though I was not wearing a badge with the police department, I did wear a badge and a gun and actually met one of the survivors of domestic violence. I'll never forget her face in those pictures. You know that feeling deep down in your core being that the universe had this planned all along? Yeah, it was like that. After years of abuse by my mother and stepfather as a child, I vowed at eight years old when the Christmas tree came tearing down that I would be a police officer. I was going to rescue all the little kids in abusive homes. I did not want any kids ever to see and feel what I felt protecting my little sister and brother. I did not want any little girls left in a molesting home. I did not want any kids beat so badly they could not go to school. It might have only been a short time, but I achieved my goal. I stopped the cycle for some women and saved some traumatized kids… sigh.

After 18 months of going back and forth to Northern California to visit my kids, I had enough money and moved back to California. I then hired an attorney to get custody. Going to court against a cop is a nightmare, to say the very least. The system is rigged and works against you when you are simply a civilian. Tim's mediator picked a woman who granted me custody, but Tim refused to deliver them to me. He complained that the mediator was biased and asked for a new mediation with a man. I was again granted custody, yet he still refused to give them up. I called his Commanding Officer to report that Tim has broken a court order. You see, he did not want to pay child support. So, I agreed that he would not pay me directly but would pay for their sports or any extra things they might need and the medical insurance.

It took a little over a year to get my kids home to me. They wanted to come home to me. We were together again. It was healing again near water, the American River. And to have your kids say they are proud of you certainly makes your heart swell.

My message to women like me is never to never give up. Stand in faith and fight like hell! Create your own hand-picked beautiful family so you can cut the natal bonds of horror. Step away from anyone or anything that does not help you radiate your bright, shiny light.

Sometimes we have to get down and dirty to concur the dark dragons. Focus on your goal, your end game, the results that you will manifest. Life can be beautiful, and you just have to decide to make it so. I will always draw from the sacred silver well. Blessed Be.

Annie Redwolf Murphy

8

Crumble and Rise
RELEASING TRAUMA

"The most courageous decision that you can make is to be in a good mood."
Voltaire

I had a crush on a boy at school who seemed to notice everyone but me. So, when he asked me to hang out, I was so excited. It was a professional day at school, and I had plans to meet a friend at the mall. He told me to stop by on my way there.

When I got there, he turned on a movie, and we cuddled on the couch, and he started to touch me. At first, I was flattered that he liked me, but it quickly escalated to a situation where I was uncomfortable and wanted him to stop. It went from him being my first kiss to him wanting to have sex with me. He did not stop and my shouts of "NO" went unheard, and he raped me.

After it happened, I got dressed and asked him why he would do that and why he wouldn't listen to me. He proceeded to the fridge, took out yogurt, and leaned against the counter, laughing at me eating his yogurt. I couldn't believe this was happening and I ran to the bus stop and continued to the mall. I didn't know what to do or how to process what just happened. I would make eye contact with strangers on the bus and wished they knew what I just went through. I remember thinking they have no idea what just happened to me.

I arrived at the mall and sat on a bench while I waited for my friend to arrive. A lady approached me and asked me to stand up, so I did. She handed me a business card and said my height would make me a great model and I should give her office a call. I had no idea how this happened when I was replaying what had just happened to me over and over. My friend showed up, and I didn't say anything. We went about our business as two teenage girls do at a mall.

I went home that evening, and there were messages on my family's message machine from my friends at school. They were calling me all types of nasty names because the boy who had assaulted me told them that we had sex, and I regretted it, so I would tell everyone he raped me. One of my friends liked this boy, and now I was the slut for sleeping with him because she liked him and couldn't believe I would do that to her. I guess she thought I wanted to sleep with him and tried to do it behind her back.

They would not stop calling, and my parents had to unplug the phone because they would not stop. Each time they called, they would say nasty things about me on leaving messages for everyone in my family to hear. I had two younger siblings in the house, and my parents didn't want them to hear the horrible messages, so they unplugged the answering machine. They asked me why all of this was happening, and I said that I had got into a fight with one of my friends, and now they were ganging up on me. I didn't know how to tell them what really had happened.

Before the assault, I was struggling with depression and had been cutting myself to numb the pain. Since a child, I always found it hard to be happy. I didn't enjoy playing with kids doing the normal things that kids do. I preferred to be alone, reading, or hanging out with adults. That night I pulled out the scissors and tried to numb the over-whelming pain by cutting my skin. It wasn't enough to stop what happened from replaying repeatedly, and I needed this terrible feeling to stop. I then took a handful of anti-anxiety pills. I suffered from anxiety, and I had them for the times where I couldn't calm myself down. I was hoping to drift off to sleep and forget about what had happened. It scared me once the pills were in my system that this could be the end, I could feel myself getting sleepy, and it scared me, so I called 911.

I went and woke my parents up and told them the ambu-lance was on the way because I had taken some pills. Of course, my parents were scared, and they didn't want the ambulance showing up and our neighbors wondering what was going on. I also had younger siblings, and I'm sure they didn't want to explain what was happening to them as they wouldn't understand. They sat with me, and we waited for the ambulance to arrive. I explained to them that I was fighting with a friend at school, and I just wanted to end the pain. The ambulance took me to the hospital. I was kept there to be monitored. I didn't mention anything that had happened as I didn't know how to say what had happened. I was still in disbelief that someone I knew could hurt me like that.

The weekend went by, and I returned to school on Monday. A lady who worked at my school in a counselor-type role, who I was familiar with, came to me before school started and said she had heard a rumor that I slept with this boy over the weekend. I told her that I had said no, and he didn't listen. She took me into her office and explained that it is a big deal and was not okay, and I need to tell my parents if that was the case. She spoke with the principal, and they called my parents, and my mom came to the school to pick me up. I was then taken to the hospital to perform a rape kit.

When my mom and I returned home from the hospital, my dad had received a phone call while we were gone. The boy who had raped me had called my dad and told him I was lying. My dad asked me if I was sure that this had happened, and I assured him that it had.

I didn't return to that school again. I was put into a program where someone coordinates my schoolwork between the teachers and brings it to me at home. I finished the remainder of school from home and lost most of my friends.

The following year I went to a new school. I was hoping for a fresh start with my sister and one friend I had left in town. My story had reached this school already, and there were rumors had started about me. I refused to meet new people for the fear that I would be rejected and bullied again. I arranged with the school principal to pick up my work in the morning from my teachers, complete it in the library, return my finished work the same day, and head home early. I was petrified of being judged or told I was lying about what happened. I never wanted to be questioned or judged again, so I did everything possible to prevent that.

That same year, the boy who raped me died. There were articles in the paper when he died, and my new school even held an event in memory of him. I could not believe he got to leave this world early and that I was stuck here in pain. I was stuck here listening to everyone say how it was so sad that he had died so young when he had already killed me inside. I graduated a semester early and started working full-time. I was not too fond of school and found no reason to be there any longer than I needed to be.

Shortly after the rape, I was introduced to an older boy by a friend. He was so nice and never tried to touch me. I felt so safe and secure with him. He became the only person I wanted to be around and the only person I would let close to me. I thought it was true love and that I should sacrifice everything to earn his trust and commitment. I just wanted him to love me and keep me safe. I was with him for seven years, and it was a long seven years of loving someone who lied, cheated, and manipulated me. When I met him, he was such a gentleman. He didn't try to sleep with me, he would drive me places, and I thought he was the nicest person ever.

As our relationship progressed, I found out he had a girl-friend. He would tell me they had broken up, and then I would find out they hadn't. She eventually left him, and I thought he had picked me, and I was the one he wanted. But over time, he did to me what he did to her. He was seeing other girls behind my back, putting the girl's numbers in his phone as guy's numbers. We went on vaca-tion, and he took out all of the photos of us together to prove he was single. I didn't understand why he couldn't love me, and I did everything I could to earn his love, but the back and forth and tension between my family and being with someone like him, I had had enough. After years of my depression running my life and losing every job I had due to my depression and rocky relationship, it was over, and we were done for good.

I bought my condo, thinking this would be the motivation I needed to get it together. I was 22 and in my place with a new job and wanted to be proud of the life I lived. I couldn't quite keep it together, though. I was trying all types of different medications to help with my depression, but nothing was working. I attempted suicide again, and at that point, I had lost my job and was behind on mortgage payments. My parents insisted I rent my condo out and move in with them. I found someone to rent my place, and I moved into my parent's home.

This was something I would go back and forth with for a few years after. I continued to date men who treated me poorly. I gained a lot of weight and gave up on taking care of myself. I would get jobs, and my depression would contribute to me missing days and lying about why until I was forced to quit or was fired. I couldn't quite get it right. I never felt good enough to date someone who would actually contribute to a healthy relationship. Why would someone with a career and a good life want someone who can't keep a job and is depressed all the time? I found it more comfortable to hang out with guys similar to me, no real job, no ambition, and tons of issues, just like me.

Reading the paper one day while living with my parents, I read an ad in the newspaper for a makeover challenge. It was a group of women getting together to make changes in their lives, which could work for me. I joined and met many great women and had a lot of inspiration and support around me. It sparked a love for the gym, and I started to feel better about myself.

My weight started to change. I gave up on dating for a bit and tried to be okay with myself. I stopped all antidepressants and did everything I could to try and feel better. I knew that if I had felt that bad for so long, it couldn't get any worse, and it was worth a shot. The energy it would take to change couldn't be any more than the energy it took every day to justify my self-destructive behaviors. I realized I am the only person responsible for my reality, and I need to start taking responsibility for my life.

When I was ready to date, I met someone who I thought was a great match. I thought I was good enough for him, which was a great feeling as I never went for anyone who I thought would actually be worth it. I always went for guys who needed me to fix them, men who needed love, someone I could improve and feel good about myself after. This guy didn't need anything from me, and that made me feel like maybe this was the right one. I was wrong. He was not suitable at all, and it got to the point where I had to ask myself what I was doing and why I was continuing to get myself into these situations.

I was hit with a problem where I realized I had to rise above or everything would crumble. I could no longer be stuck in this cycle selling myself short and blaming others for my shitty situations. I had been in and out of counseling since I was in my pre-teens. I would be committed to finding growth and learn to cope with my past to thinking I didn't need it and had everything figured out. I found out that because I had been raped and filed a police report that I was eligible for counseling paid for through victim's services. I started counseling and began processing my trauma and all the ways it had altered me and how to start moving towards health again.

A fantastic job came available. I applied for my dream job and got an interview. At the interview, I was asked what the hardest thing I had to do in my life was? I knew I couldn't answer that truthfully. What I had just gone through and walked away from wasn't something you share with two strangers at an interview for your dream job. I made up an answer of how selling my condo was the hardest decision. That's not far off from the truth, but it wasn't exactly true either.

The day of this interview, my life was crumbling from another failed relationship that left me so emotionally scarred I didn't think I'd ever recover. I knew, though, that if I didn't go to this interview and give it my all, bad things would continue to happen. I would be so disappointed in myself to let another good opportunity go by because I was bathing in my self-pity.

I got the job. And I am still at that job. I love it and am so grateful for it every day. I work with people with who I can be myself. I finally got stable enough that I moved out of my parents into my own home again and juggled work, gym, bills, and my personal life. I've got to a place where I am happy to sit by myself, and didn't require medication anymore. I was okay not being surrounded by distractions to keep me from acknowledging the trauma flowing inside my body. I met someone who lived in my building, and we started dating. We have now been together for a few years, and we have a baby together.

I am so grateful for not giving up and for choosing myself. Once I accepted that I was responsible for my life, the good and the bad, things got better. It was so challenging to admit that my choices had brought me to a place I was unhappy in, but with that, it also meant I was in control of making the changes to get me too somewhere where I am happy. And I have found that happy place inside me today.

For those of you who may be struggling, don't keep quiet about something traumatic that might have happened to you. Please don't be silent. You owe it to yourself to speak up. Step up and get the help you might need. I finally did that, which helped me move forward to a positive place in my life. My happy place.

Cheyenne Williams

9

Never Say Never
MY STORY OF SURPRISES

**"My mama always said, life is like a box of chocolates.
You never know what you're gonna get."**
Forrest Gump

On a stairwell, on a sunny day, I watched my brother laugh as I cried uncontrollably. He had just stolen my nose and threw it in the trunk he was sitting on. I begged him to give it back, and he refused, giggling that I would never get it back. That's when two of my older sisters came to see why I was crying. I told them how Wayne, our brother, stole my nose and wouldn't give it back through my sobs. They too laughed and kept saying it was on my face; how could it be when I saw my brother take it from my face and throw it in the trunk. They left me to face my brother on my own, to deal with my own battle.

He eventually gave it back, and that is how at three, I learned that not everyone has your back.

Isn't that what life really is? A journey of lessons, chapters of where you learn life's lessons. Some are universal, and some are very personal. Here are mine, good or bad, they just are, and I would like to share them with you.

Chapter one Birth to 18.

I consider this the first chapter in my life. Lots happened during that time that shaped who I was to become and my choices in my later years (chapters). So for some background, I am the youngest of six, five girls, and one brother. My parents had me late in life and several years after my next-in-line sister. They didn't think they could get pregnant due to their age and my Mom's uterus being tilted and having only one ovary. My Mom was 38, and my Dad was 63 when they found out they were pregnant with me. Needless to say, I was a surprise baby but also a loved and wanted baby.

Unfortunately, I never got to know my Dad. He died not even two years later, at age 65, basically of old age. He was born in 1906 in South Africa, where my Mom met him, and he died here in Canada in May of 1972, two months before my second birthday. His death and absence in my life impacted me, whether I was aware of it or not. I knew at a very young age that he died and that he loved me very much. I knew ALL about him, but I never KNEW him. Looking back, would my life have been different had he not died when I was so young? Would my choices have been different? Would the things that happened to me as a child not have happened had he lived longer?

I remember my childhood as a happy one, I grew up with our dog Sassy, and she was just another sibling. I have only one memory or memories of my childhood that really affected my choices growing up, the ones that formed me. That would be my brother sexually abusing me from when I was four to age nine—the same brother who stole my nose. Looking back, he was just a child himself, only 14 when the abuse started. I ended it at age nine by simply saying, " I don't want to play Mommy & Daddy anymore." He never asked again, and I hid that part of my life for five years!

Every interaction with my brother between ages nine and 14 was strained, and I couldn't figure out why. I just thought it was because he was so much older, and I didn't know him that well. I had nothing but good things to say about him. He paid me an allowance from seven to nine years old. He worked with the horses at the Hasting Race-course in Vancouver, and we visited him often there, where he showed us the horses. Looking back, I get why he gave me a weekly allowance and why our relationship was strained. However, I had horrible recurring nightmares of demons trying to enter a bathroom I was in during those years. And somehow, I always managed to close the door. They felt so real, too and one morning at the age of 14, waking up from one of these nightmares, I realized it was a memory. It wasn't a demon, it was my brother, and somehow the bathroom was where it started.

It was years later that I told anyone about it, as I felt shame. I remembered the first time it happened and the last time. And the last time was where I felt the shame, as I had ended it. And because I ended it, I could have ended it at any time. So I told no one. This memory and the abuse itself shaped how I felt about sex and love now as an adult. Had my Dad been alive, would this have happened? Would my choices have been different? I don't know, and don't dwell on it too much because the what-ifs in life can drive you crazy.

By the time I was 15, I had become sexually active, and here is where I discovered guys like girls who give it up. And when I gave it up, I felt love, and strangely enough, I was never really present when I had sex. I would go off somewhere in my head, never having any kind of intimacy. Just sex, so of course, I was promiscuous. I had sex with guys my age, older, and some twice my age. If I found them slightly attracted, I was having sex even if I didn't feel like it. Looking back, I didn't know how to say no. To be honest, I had no clue that was even an option. It wasn't in my vocabulary. I eventually learned it, but it took having my son and being a call girl to get there.

A great Segway to the next chapter in my life.

Chapter Two 18 -25

By the time I hit 18, I had had a few boyfriends. Most were older. So when I met Jamie, who was four months younger, to me, he was just a f**k buddy. A very fun f**k buddy and a good friend. However, at the same time, I had been dating a 23-year-old naval seaman, Allan, in Victoria. So when I became pregnant, I first told Jamie and also that I wasn't keeping it. But then I remembered my time with Allan and realized it had to be his. I was back and forth from New Westminster, where Jamie was, to Victoria, where Allan was. After discussing with my Mom, I decided to keep the baby and move back to Victoria to live with my eldest sister. I also confronted Allan, who denied it was his, saying it was impossible as he had a vasectomy at age 17. This was a lie as he did go on to have other children.

I had my son a week before my 19th birthday, and I raised him on my own. When my son was four months old, I moved back to Chilliwack, where I grew up. I haven't mentioned it yet, and I should. Growing up in Chilliwack, I was a Jehovah's Witness. I was what they called "born into the truth." So when I moved back there at age 19, I ran into people I had grown up with as a JW. Eventually, I started going back to meetings at the Kingdom Hall and was baptized.

This was also a time of great depression for me. I was lonely, I was angry, and I felt so very alone. I was so despondent at one point, and I was seriously contemplating suicide. The only thing stopping me was that I couldn't think of a way to end my life and not affect my son Zak's life. I was on many antidepressants, and they were not working for me either. I realized that I had a lot of anger towards my brother, and that is where most of my depression stemmed from. I had so much hate towards him that I wished him dead.

Before it got better, my Mom called one September after-noon to inform me that my brother had died from a heroin overdose. My brother had been addicted to heroin since he was about 18. However, he was a rare functional addict. He was constantly employed, mainly as a drywaller. My brother was 33 when he passed. I was 23 and had just wished him dead a month earlier. Well, my wish came true, but I felt like shit! I thought I was supposed to be happy. Why the fucking am I grieving his death??? Man, was I ever messed up.

Several days later, after this news, with my brain short-circuiting over how I should feel about his death and all the conflicting feelings I was having, my son and I were invited to lunch at an older woman's home, a JW sister. I may not remember her name, but I am forever grateful for her. While being there, she asked how I was doing as she knew about my brother's death. Well, that was all I needed to let it all pour out, the tears, the grief, the love, and the whole confusion over it all!

She listened to me intently, with love and no judgments. Then she freed me from the chains I put on myself. She gave me the permission I needed to be my authentic self.

She said," Laurene, it's okay to love your brother. It's okay to grieve him! Hate what he did to you. You don't have to hate him." WOW! Those words are forever burned into my soul! I thought I had to hate him. I didn't know love was an option.

I learned that that day, Love and Forgiveness are ALWAYS an option. I loved my brother, and I never stopped loving him. I still cherish the few letters we wrote to each other. He was a child himself when the abuse started. He was a troubled man, and I have forgiven him, and I genuinely hope that he found some peace in death.

I made peace with my brother a long time ago, it wasn't overnight, but I'm grateful I have been able to.

This was the beginning of the end of me being a JW. I wasn't happy, and I didn't fit in. I was a single Mom, and I didn't fit in the narrative. I wasn't widowed, divorced, etc. So I had nothing in common with that group. The single's my age couldn't relate to me as they had no kids. The couples with kids, well, I was always the third wheel, same with the couples without kids. It sure didn't help my depression, and it was a pretty lonely time for me. I decided to move closer to my Mom and Step-Dad and moved to Mission.

When I first moved there, I continued going to JW meetings. It wasn't for me, on so many levels, even with a new congregation. And with members I had gone to school with, who were surprised and supportive even. I was still that single Mom with the kid. I still felt very ostracized. It wasn't intentional, but like before, I didn't fit into their narrative. No matter where I went, it was the older widowed woman with whom I got paired up with. I was 23, and as much as I loved older women in their 50's and up, I needed to be around people of my own age. And that my friend was one of the main reasons I stopped going to meetings.

Then I started hanging out with the heathens, my awesome neighbors in the fourplex where I lived: Donalda and her sister. Donalda lived above me and her sister lived on the other side on the top. We weren't great friends, but we got along and enjoyed being neighbors.

This was when my life became very interesting. I had newfound freedom. I was young, alone, and I was horny! I had been celibate for close to three years, and it was time to break the seal.

So being the mid 90's there is no internet. I live in a small town with no nightlife. I just stopped going to church. So how did one meet new people then? It was called Phone Dating. Free for women and men had to pay. Not unlike its successor, Internet Dating. You made a profile, had a paragraph about you, and you scrolled through the male profiles. The only difference was it was all verbal and no pictures. You thought you got catfished on internet dating? Let me tell you, it was as prolific on phone chat as it was called. I thought it would have been better when I got into internet dating ten years later, but no, you still get catfished.

So back in 1994, with this new phone chat, I started meeting men again and again was pretty promiscuous. I still hadn't learned the word "no" or even "hey; let's wait" either. I wouldn't say I was dating but definitely having several sexual encounters. It was then that I met two men. One became a friend and the other a catalyst for something I never thought I would do in my whole life but looking back, and I was a perfect candidate.

I eventually met this great English guy named Ramen. We were not sexually attracted to each other, but we definitely were attracted intellectually. He was a good friend, never steered me wrong, and also pointed out the consequences. This was when I was propositioned by the catalyst, an older man that wanted to meet me but had a strange request. He wanted me to touch myself in front of him in my underwear, and after I had reached my height of pleasure, he wanted my underwear.

At 24, I thought I was sophisticated, I was worldly, but OMG, that shocked me. And I realized there was a whole world out there with people that had, um, let us say, unique ways that made them happy.

At first, I said no, but he kept leaving messages on my phone chat profile inbox. At one point, he said he'd pay me $75 for the experience. I was immediately offended. Who did this guy think I was? A prostitute, how rude! I mentioned this casually to my friend Ramen, and he was like, why not? You're out there doing it might as well get paid for it. And it's not like you're having sex with him. I saw his point, and so I agreed. He did give me a warning, " Do it for fun and NEVER EVER do it for money."

The panty man contacts me again, and this time I agreed, along with the payment. Once he left, I was super stoked. That was the easiest $75 bucks I ever made in my life! As a single Mom on Welfare in 1995, that was a lot of money and bought many groceries and extra things I wouldn't usually buy, being I was always strapped for cash.

I told Ramen of the experience and how easy it was and why didn't I think of it blah blah blah. That's when he gave me the above warning and said it could suck me into a dark place. I assured him, " I got this!!"

Also, during my exploration of sexual me, I met another man who introduced me to S & M. Before I met him, I always thought of myself as a bottom, the submissive one. I told him as much and that I was really curious to explore that side of me. In my first encounter with him, I learned VERY quickly I was NO bottom. I believe 20 minutes into it, I looked at him and said, " if you say one more thing or smack my ass one more time, I swear that will be the last time you'll use that hand or speak out of your mouth!!" He laughed, which made me want to punch him in the face even more. Shaking his head, " I didn't think you were a bottom, but I figured I would let you find out for yourself."

Well, well, I was learning more about myself every day, and that of my friends, when my exploration into becoming a call girl and a dominatrix (Mistress Amy) began.

On the surface, however, I wanted to do something completely different with my life. I wanted to become a youth counselor. I had been volunteering at the local Youth Center, and after meeting the youth counselors there, it seemed like a good fit. I researched and found that Douglas College in New Westminster had a program, and I met the entrance requirements. The only problem was the distance, I lived in Mission, and well back in the late '90s, there was no actual transit to the Greater Vancouver area, and even though the West Coast Express had started running, logistically, it didn't work. So the decision was made to move to New Westminster, with plans to go to college and have a career. A career I did have but not quite that one I was expecting. Funny how life throws you curveballs.

Chapter 3 25-27.

In1996 my son and I moved into a one-bedroom apt, he was six, and we lived within walking distance to an elementary school. I was also within walking distance to the college, which I fully expected to attend in six months.

Life had other plans! Being in the city meant men were more accessible, and more men were interested in meeting me as I now lived closer. And when I say meeting me, I mean in a paid sexual way. I was charging $150 an hour and, for every half hour after the first hour, $50. On average, I was making $200 every time. I didn't do it every day, but I would say 1-2 times a week on average. As a Mom on welfare, it was significant extra cash. Zak would be in school, and I'd be working. By combining my newfound Mistress Amy to the paid sex worker trade, I also learned that I could charge twice as much and not even have sex. Like HELLO!!! Where do I sign up??

This was the upside of being a call girl/dominatrix, the money, the control. The feeling of pride that men were paying me the privilege to have sex with me and or have me dominate them. There was a downside, and it took me a while to see it. I felt it, but I was used to feeling disheartened in life, and I just thought, here we go again.

However, during the upside part, I developed a clientele. Some were just there for the sex, some for the kink, and some for both. I also had a broker, I never met him, but we did have many conversations. He had high-end business clients visiting Vancouver for business and wanted sex with no hassle. So every once in a while, he'd call me up, and we'd make arrangements. Only once I said no, I knew who he was, my kid knew who he was, my God, most kids in Canada knew who he was. AND that my friend did not feel right. Confidentiality stops me from naming the person, but I'll never forget how naive I felt at that moment. I had pondered how could someone that kids look up to want a call girl? I had forgotten we're all human and have needs.

During all this time "working," I developed a taste for cocaine. A lot of my clients did it and brought it over to do with me. I had one repeat customer who paid me for my time as we never had sex but just got together to get high on coke. He always had coke and lots of it, well, being a dealer that dealt only in the kilos. It made sense. I imagine he did very well as he drove a blue Rolls Royce. For Christmas that year, he gifted me almost half a kilo of coke. That lasted me a long time. I never sold it. I kept it for myself. Due to this practically never-ending supply, I was up to having seven lines for breakfast every day.

This is where life started to become dark for me, I was high all the time, and I began to hate being a dominatrix. It felt like work, and I started to hate the men that came to me. I thought they were losers and wimpy pussy's that couldn't stand up for themselves. So I needed to stop because I was not respecting them nor myself. I hated being a call girl. I felt so degraded that men were paying me for sex. But I liked the money, and I hated myself for continuing it because of the money it brought in. I was lonely, depressed, and felt like such an imposter. I only felt normal when I was high, which is why I did so much of it. When I was high, I felt like an adult, like a Mom should, weirdly enough. When I wasn't high, I felt like a child.

After two years of being a call girl, seven to nine months approximately of being a dominatrix, and almost six or more months of being constantly high, my world crashed around me. At the beginning of this journey or chapter of my life, I was confident, in control, and now I was a wreck. Depressed, I couldn't face anyone without being high. This included my Mom. I had done things that I regretted and wasn't proud of. Especially for neglecting my son, I thought I was there, but I wasn't present in reality, even if my body was. I needed help, and I knew I messed up, and my son needed help too.

So here begins my new chapter 27-32.

To get the help I needed, I moved to Abbotsford to be near my Mom. My son was now in a foster home so I could get clean and receive counseling. I needed to work on myself to be the Mom my son needed me to be. I believed being in Abbotsford was a great step. By not being close to the Metro Vancouver area, my clients were not going to travel, and neither was I.

Who knew that Abbotsford was a drug hub, and the apartment my Mom found for me was prostitute central? I for sure didn't, though it didn't take long for me to find out. Whether I was walking back from getting cigarettes at the nearby store or just getting off the bus from grocery shopping, I was constantly propositioned. I said no for the first little while, but I hated being broke, so I gave in.

Even though I was going to college to get a computer admin degree, I was hooking and doing coke again, falling back into the old habits. That's when I met him, my literal knight in shining armor. He started as a client, but he would just call me and ask me to hang out with him and his friends after the second time. A little backstory of my knight, he was a drug dealer, and we would hang out in this empty house that he had a key for—basically a drug den party house. We called it the party house.

One night sitting in his car waiting for him to take me home as I had school the following day, he was stalling. He wanted me to stay longer. He was trying to convince me to stay the whole time, he had all these other girls calling him, and I said as much. He told me they meant nothing to him, and that's when it hit me, He LIKES ME! He really, really likes me! He denied it a few times, but finally, he admitted he did. Then this is when he became my knight in shining armor, even if I didn't see it at the time. He became very serious and told me I was too nice to be doing what I had been doing. That I needed to stop, and he would help me financially if that's what it would take for me to stop. Basically, he saw my worth, me, I had no clue what my worth was, but this man saw it and wanted me to see it. He kept his word about supporting me; mind you, it was drug money he made at the party house. I was to keep all tender he received of $10 and under. So he kept all the tender of $20 bills and more. I would keep all the $10, $5, and change. I was making more with Jag than I did hooking. For the time, it was a great trade-off.

But let me tell you about Jag. This man built me up! Through his help and vision, I went from a drug-addicted prostitute to a woman with purpose! I was worthy, and he never let me forget my worth. If I expressed any doubt, he was there to remind me. He also helped me get my first "real" job in years at a wholesale nursery. Once I was laid off there, he steered me to sales, so I started working at Moore's clothing for men, where I made my way up to Assistant Manager. And from that position, I went on to manage Jag's men's clothing store that he decided to open.

Along the way, Jag and I fell in love! I was introduced to his family, his Mom and Dad. We were together for just over six years. I wanted to marry him, but I was white and an ex-prostitute. I didn't think my past had anything to do with my present, but then again, I dealt with a different culture as Jag was Punjabi. His family wasn't ever going to accept me as an option. I see that now but then I was blinded by love. Almost two years before we parted ways, he went on a trip to India, and when he came back, I knew something was up. He tried to avoid me at first, then he came to my place and full-on cried. His heart was broken, and all he could say was that his family didn't want him to be with me, but he loved me, but his family was more to him than I was. So he was torn. He failed to tell me that he was married, which was the reason for the trip to India. I found that out months later, he had just said he was engaged.

During this time, I found out that I was pregnant. In fact, this was the third time I had become pregnant with Jag. One was a miscarriage, the second a morning-after pill. And here I was pregnant again, again on the pill, but I kind of wanted the baby this time. Jag did not, but I was unsure. However, after a long talk with myself and contemplating what life might look like with this child, I decided that perhaps an abortion was the best thing at that time. It was not the easiest of choices in my life nor the worst. I don't regret the abortion, but I sure did grieve her. I knew she was a girl, I was only six weeks along, but I knew.

A few months after the abortion, we ended our relationship. He found out that his wife (who had left him after realizing I was still in his life, I don't blame her, and I don't know what I was thinking) had had his son. That's when he decided to be with her and be a husband. At that point, I was okay with it. It had been over for a while for me, and he had fallen in love with his son. I had let him go. We parted amicably, well we had one fight. He told me that I should have kept that baby. The one he told me he didn't want. I slapped him so hard my hand stung, and I walked away and went home. I didn't talk to him for two days. I had been helping him pack for his move to Brampton when he told me this. Those words hurt me. If he had said at the time that he might have wanted the baby to, I would have kept it. When I did finally return his call, he apologized. Before moving, we made up, and he presented me with an almost engagement-type ring. It was a 22 kt gold ring with a large amethyst surrounded by six sizeable diamonds.

When he left, I knew he was only meant to be in my life for a short time, but he gave me so much, and I am forever grateful that I met him. He was my knight. He came and rescued me from myself. He will always have a part of me, and I hold space for him in my heart always.

Last ongoing chapter 33 to present

So here I was, single again, working a reasonably decent job and kind of dating but more like one-night stands. This time I knew what I wanted. I wanted a f**k buddy and was enjoying auditioning the men, even if they didn't know it. I wasn't ready to be in another relationship but still wanted companionship.

And that's how I got pregnant at 32. Gahhh, I was on the pill, taking it religiously, and yet again, I got pregnant. Like really? Sigh. I found out I was pregnant precisely nine months after the abortion, and I could not do that again. So I decided to move forward with the pregnancy. I didn't want to do it alone. The father, aka sperm donor, decided he had too many kids with too many other women. Can we say red flags? I knew there was a reason he was a one-night stand. However, here I was, single and pregnant. So at age 33, I had a baby girl in Feb of 2005, 15 ½ years after my son.

When my daughter was eight months old, I moved back to Chilliwack. In four months, I would be going back to work, and since my work was there and one of my sisters who also lived there had agreed to be my daycare provider, it made sense. Once I was settled in, and about a month before, I went back to work. I was ready to date again, so since it was 2006, online dating it was. I met a few duds and was catfished a few times before noticing this handsome man had messaged me. His online tag was Volbek. He was my age, had a lot of the same interests and bonus he lived in Chilliwack.

After a few messages back and forth, we phoned each other and set up a date night. It ended up being at my place as my babysitter fell through. So this good-looking man named James shows up, and right away, we have an instant connection. As soon as I opened the door and let him in, I felt like I'd known him all my life, and he told me he felt like he knew me too.

Against my better judgment, we end up in my bed, and he stays for breakfast. By this time in my life, I had learned the word no, and let's wait, but it felt right for whatever reason. When I woke up the following day, he was still asleep, and he had his arm around me, and it felt like home. Something I never experienced in my life, not even in the six years with Jag. Was it love at first sight? Perhaps.

When he finally woke up, he said the most peculiar thing: "You're South African, right?". No, I'm not, but my Dad is from South Africa. AND how the hell do you know that??

We made breakfast together, he met my daughter, and after he left, I KNEW not only would I be hearing from him again, but we would also be seeing each other. And that we did.

During the first few weeks of dating him, strange and weird coincidences started to happen. For instance, after hanging out with my son Zak I would go out on a date with James, and James would say word for word what my son said earlier in the day. It would also happen vice versa. I also started noticing they made the same faces when perplexed or being goofy. I began to feel I was dating my son!

So after about three weeks of this, I decided that it was too weird, and there had to be something immoral and ethically wrong with dating a man exactly like your son. We had a date set up for him to come over for dinner, and that was when I decided to end it with him and tell him why.

After we had dinner and few drinks, my girl was in bed for the night, and before I could start a conversation about why I wanted to stop dating him, he sees my photo albums. Thankful for the distraction, how do you tell a man you're dating, and everything is incredible? "Sorry, I can't see you anymore cause you're just like my son!" Can you say awkward!

As we are flipping through the photos, he comes across a picture of me at around 17. He turns to me and exclaims, " I know you!!". He became all animated and stands up and again exclaims, "I know you!!". He then describes my life in New Westminster with my best friend Michelle back when I was 18. I was like, OMG! And my brain at first was like, okay, which guy is this? I knew a lot of guys back then. He kept babbling on about things in my past with Michelle when a light bulb went off in my head, and it clicked! To confirm who I thought it was, I asked him, " You sold ciga-rettes out of the back of your car, right?" He confirmed, and that is when we stood there staring at each other with our mouths agape.

At the same time, we both came to the same conclusion; Zak's was his son! We both sat down with memories of that time flooding back. It was as if time in our lives was stamped out, and we now were reliving every moment. We were both excited to know why we felt such an instant connection to each other! And I was utterly relieved as to why Zak and James were so much alike. It all made sense now. We decided not to tell Zak until after they met each other. We still weren't 100% sure, but deep down, we knew. Approximately two months later, James was ready to meet Zak.

Zak was all nonchalant as he was just meeting Mom's new boyfriend and James was nervous as hell to meet his poten-tial son for the first time. Once Zak left to meet his friends, James immediately turned to me and said, " I'm 100 % sure that he is my son". I agreed wholeheartedly.

It blew my mind. Here is this man that I have fallen in love with, and he's my son's father. How strange, beautiful and serendipitous it all was. Before meeting James, Zak had been inquiring about his Dad and how to find him. And here he was under our nose the whole time. James and I decided to get a DNA test to make it official, and we told Zak, who was ecstatic. We received the results on June 6, 2006, which showed James as 99.99% as the father. We knew, but it was nice to make it official.

I could end my story here, everything wonderful and full of rainbows and skittles. But that isn't life, and we never know what happens tomorrow.

36-Present.

James and I are still together, and a lot has happened since that day 15 years ago. Our son is married, and James and Zak have a strained, if almost no, relationship at all. They are a lot alike and have butted heads more than not. I used to be their buffer, but I realized I couldn't interfere with their relationship. It is their relationship, not mine. As much as it hurts that they don't have this amazing relationship, it's not my business to force it either. James will say it doesn't bother him, but I know better. My son and I aren't that close either. Nor my 16-year daughter and me. She lives with my sister, which is another story altogether and would fill a book.

James and I have had many ups and downs in our relationship. We have fought, broke up, and rekindled a few times. But what brings us back together is that we are best friends, and life without each other would just be dull. No one could ever fill the void that would be there should one of us be gone.

Did my life did not turn out the way I envisioned it? No! However, I have many things in my life that I never dreamed I would have. Life is constantly changing and throwing curveballs. Some are your fault, and some are just crazy circumstances. Such as finding out two years ago I have MS (crazy curveball), but within each chapter of my life, I've learned some valuable lessons.

As a child, I learned that you could only rely on yourself. That sex was love, and love was sex. I realized that you could revisit your old life in your twenties, but that doesn't mean you have to stay. That God is everywhere you are, and he will find a way to help you heal even if you don't realize that you need healing.

I learned about men and a lot about myself. Looking back on me being a Dominatrix, I see that was a healing time for me also. All that anger about Dad dying before I could know him, my brother sexually abusing me, and subsequent abandonment issues, I took it out on men who paid me the privilege. As a call girl, I learned a lot about how men tick and why they cheat. How they love and why some find solace in a stranger's embrace.

By the time I hit my 30's I had learned about love, real love. About being intimate and present in that love. I learned about my worth, how fortunate I am, and my white privilege, which I never fully understood until then. I learned about a whole other culture and religion and the beauty in it. AND that God is everywhere. I also learned that love is sometimes not forever, and that's okay.

This last chapter in my life, well, you never stop learning new things about yourself. You're constantly changing. You are the author of your life, do things that your future self will be happy for. Curveballs are scary, and it's okay that they hit you. You can't catch them all, but ducking is an option. I've also learned at age 50, if you still don't feel like an adult at this age, no worries as long as you pay your way. Maturity isn't for everyone. Be you at all times, never stretch the truth and tell the absolute truth to everyone. How people handle it is not your business, it's theirs. You don't need to protect them.

I have learned to be grateful that my MS is more annoying than debilitating. I've also learned that never say never, I own my home, and I NEVER thought in a million years I would.

BUT then again, I never thought I'd be a call girl, a dominatrix, or meet my best friend twice. Have two children 15 years apart, have two abortions, and meet the beautiful people who were part of my journey.

We may know where we've been, but tomorrow is an unknown path, and my journey is not over, and each day is a paragraph in a new chapter.

Laurene Johansson

10

Stronger Than Yesterday

MY JOURNEY WITH MENTAL ILLNESS

"You never know how STRONG you are until being strong is the only choice."
Bob Marley

1997 is where it all began. It's the year I lost who I was as a child and who I was becoming as a person. This was when my mental health issues began. The year I met my biological father (if you can even call him a father). How can one event have such an impact on one's life?

I was 13 years old when I learned of him. I wanted to get to know this man; who was he? Where has he been all these years? Why was he now coming into my life? Questions I never got answered. Little did I know the impact this man would have on my life.

I remember each feeling as if it was yesterday. The feeling of his hand, undoing the buttons of my tearaways. I was so scared and frozen stiff. I didn't know what was happening. All I knew is I wanted it to stop, and I wanted to scream— the feeling of terror traveling through my body as his hand kept brushing up against my behind. I was screaming so loud, telling myself to move, until I finally found the strength to move just enough to startle him and interrupt the beginning of the scariest night of my life.

I remember lying awake, wanting to go home, as I laid next to this man with the wet and warm feeling of him soaked into my underwear. I often replay that night back in my head. Always questioning why? Why did this happen to me? What did I do wrong to deserve this? Never really getting answers, never feeling satisfied. How can one forgive or move on when they don't even understand and understand I did not. This was the beginning of my mental health decline.

Throughout my life, I never knew where I was going? No, matter what path I took or the direction I went in, it was never satisfying. It never filled the emptiness I felt inside. I didn't know what I was looking for, but I always searched for whatever it was. I know I was never really truly alone; I always had my family. Except it wasn't what I was looking for. I was trying to find myself, who I was, what I wanted. But I always felt alone, like no one could ever understand what I was going through. Then again, did I even know, did I even understand?

Three years of making choices that I wasn't always proud of. Dressing for attention, and attention I got from one guy to the next guy. Then the year 2000 arrived; I was 16 and still in search of who I was. I chose to be flirtatious because I wanted attention. But what I didn't know at the time is I was craving and looking for the wrong kind of attention. This is where Troy comes into my world of the unknown. He paid attention to me; I craved it, and he gave it to me. It made me feel whole, beautiful and wanted. I thought this is what I was looking for this entire time, and at that moment, I felt complete.

We went from kissing and cuddling to so much more than I wanted. My heart was racing; I felt like the walls were closing in on me. There was no escape, no matter how much I pleaded for him to stop. He was stronger than me, and I couldn't prevent it from happening, feeling like it was never going to end. But it was finally over. He had left, and all I could do was curl up in a ball and cry. It felt like it was all my fault that I asked for it without speaking the words.

I found out I was pregnant. I didn't know what I was going to do. I was only 16, and I wasn't ready to be a mother. I ended up having a miscarriage. The Doctor said that my body wasn't prepared for pregnancy and that it was for the best. I was so full of mixed emotions. I was angry that I was going through this and scared because I wasn't ready. I was sad because I lost the baby, and I didn't understand why; but I was happy that I didn't have to go through this alone, that it was over and I would never have to think about it again, or so I thought.

I continued on the path of questioning who I was and who I wanted to be. My emotions were a rollercoaster from one moment to the next. It was never knowing if I was coming or going. I didn't understand what was going on with me. I had already lost my virginity; I didn't think I could lose anything more at this point. The negative thoughts were always there, never wanting to leave. I wanted it to all go away, although it never did. I knew my mental health was declining.

I became depressed and so sad. This was when I was introduced to antidepressants. I tried them but never stuck with them. I didn't want to be that person who needed medication to be normal. So, I continued on my way. Three more years of making choices I wasn't always proud of, leading to three more miscarriages and an abusive relationship I never thought I would escape.

It was 2003 when Corey came into my life. I was head over heels in love. It was like being on cloud nine. I felt needed and wanted, and with every word he spoke, I was in a world where no one else existed. All those negative thoughts were slowly slipping away. I was in love.

You know that saying everyone has a story and every story is a lesson to be learned. So, what lesson was I to learn from Corey? Deep inside me, I have something that wants to save everyone or anyone who walks into my life. I try so hard to look back and see the good in what Corey and I had, but all I see is a scared, lonely girl. A girl who felt like she had nowhere or no one to turn to. I now realize that I was the one needing to be saved.

Corey was troubled and got himself into trouble. When he was locked up in jail, he still somehow had control over me. I was scared not to answer the phone, yet I was just as scared if he didn't phone me. One minute, Corey told me he was sorry, loves me, and never meant to hurt me. Then the next minute, he would be verbally and mentally abusing me. Finally, he pulled me in by painting a picture of hope, love, and happiness—one that I longed for, one that I wanted more than anything. I wanted to believe his every word, but that is all they were WORDS that would soon crush my world.

Fast forward to 2004, and my firstborn was here. He was truly my world, my everything, even though Corey still had a hold of me. I was scared to stand against him. I was afraid of what he was capable of doing. He never cared about my feelings as long as he got what he wanted. I did such horrible things for him, some things that I will have to live with forever. But I soon found my voice.

Who knew a child of my own could give me such strength and courage to walk away, to make things right? It only took three of the scariest words I ever heard Corey say, "I'LL KILL HIM," and I was gone from his life forever. His threats no longer had a hold on me. But what was the lesson to be learned?

Poor choices seem to be my path of choice, now came the time in my life that I started using drugs—my drug of choice, MDMA (best known as the love drug). The more I took it, the more I wanted it. I loved the feeling of freedom from life and my emotions, but mainly the unknown path I was on.

That is when Mike entered the next chapter in my life. Before I knew it, I was pregnant with my second child and scared. I was frightened of being a single mom of two and doing it all on my own. At first, the relationship was based on me being pregnant and being scared to be alone. As time went on, I fell in love, or so I thought. It wasn't real, though; it was a false hope of what I wanted so desperately.

I fought through 8 long years, trying to make it work. Except it was always one-sided. The other side was going down a rabbit hole of crime, drugs, and cheating. The best way to describe this man child is that he is a pathological liar with charm. Even in my heart, when I knew he was lying, he had a way of making me feel like I was in the wrong. It didn't help that I had absolutely no self-esteem. I was so desperate to have the happily ever after that I truly believed all the negative in my life.

It was the middle of the night, and I was nine months pregnant, sleeping on the couch when I woke up to a banging on the door. There stood two police officers, asking me if I knew where my car was. I explained to them that Mike and his friend had borrowed the car and should be sitting at King George Skytrain station. They then informed me that it was in a high-speed chase down my street. They then handed me a $900 ticket because they believed I knew who was in the car while it was in the high-speed chase.

Another miracle in my life was born, she was beautiful, and I could not imagine life without her. I tried day in and day out to keep pushing through life and all the negative. I wanted to protect my babies but always felt as if I was failing as a parent. I was always trying to make things right.

By 2009 I just couldn't take any more. I was done with life and the path I was on. I never finished school. I was 25 years old and felt like I had absolutely nothing to show for it. This was when I decided I didn't want to live any longer. While I held the knife in my hand pressed against my vein, reality kicked in, and I thought of my children. I had not one but two beautiful children who needed me. I contacted my Doctor, who got me into Crest Treatment Centre. It was by far the best decision I could have ever made for ME, yes me.

While I was at Crest, I learned how to care for myself and what signs and triggers I needed to watch for. I learned how to cope with life and the choices I made. I learned what made me happy. I loved to draw, write, and listen to music; these were my escapes. Eventually, I added these to my coping list.

Life was good again; my anxiety was down, and my depression was under control. Even Mike and I were doing good. So good that we planned for our third child.

Our new little baby was so chubby and cute, and I couldn't believe I now had three beautiful and amazing kids. Of course, we had our ups and downs. But we were a family, and these kids were my life, my everything. They kept me going in my darkest days, and then the dark days were back.

Mike was back to doing what he did best, drugs and crime, which led to him losing his steady full-time job. He ended up getting arrested, then managed to convince the lawyer and judge that he was the sole provider of our family. So rather than jail, he was given house arrest. Unfortunately, our relationship and Mike's behavior never got better, and I couldn't take it any longer. My mental health was going downhill fast, I saw the signs, and I did what I needed to do for my kids and me.

With help from family and friends, the kids and I temporarily moved out into a friend's apartment. I was a mom of three, working a full-time job as a flagger. I was exhausted but did what I needed to do.

One day I was working, and it was hot out. I was in the middle of an intersection when I started to feel off. I radioed my supervisor, who pulled me off the road into the shade and said I probably had heatstroke. I said I don't think so, this feels different, and I need to go to a doctor. So, I drove to the closest clinic.

They did a pregnancy test and said this would take a couple of minutes, but I swear it wasn't even 30 seconds later, and the Doctor was walking back in the room telling me I was pregnant. I had instant tears, I could barely breathe, and my anxiety was rising fast. The Doctor said, "I take it this was not planned nor expected." I explained my situation, and he told me what my options were. I told him abortion was out of the question and that there is no way I could carry this baby to term just to turn around and hand the baby over to someone else.

So, I decided I would be a mom of not three but four kids.

At this time, I informed my landlord that I had not been living in the house and explained the situation to him. He then told me that Mike had not been paying rent; it had been eight months. My jaw dropped open, the tears started to roll down my face, and I was in shock. Not that Mike had not paid rent in eight months but that the landlord had not kicked us out. He didn't know that I had taken the children and left the house. It was an incredible kindness shown to me. I stepped up and made another huge decision in my life. I sat down with my landlord and made an agreement with him to pay the back rent off month by month. I decided to move back into the house, and as for Mike and I, nothing ever changed.

I was pregnant with my 4th child, and I was mentally and emotionally exhausted. Fraser Health called to check in on me. The nurse assigned to me was a newbie and followed her script to a T, never asking why I gave the answers I did. The first few questions are a blur to me but lead to the following conversation.

Fraser Health "Would you ever harm yourself?"

Me "Yes and No"

Fraser Health "Would you ever harm your children?"

Me "Yes and No"

She then placed me on hold, and the next thing I knew, the Ministry of Children and Family Services were at my house. They gave me the option to either admit myself to the hospital, or they could remove my kids from my care. So off I went to the Emergency Room. It felt like time went by so slow – until I could talk to them and tell them why I said what I said, Why I felt the way I felt. I explained that I wanted to harm myself because of my mental health, but I wasn't going to as my kids need me. Yes, if I hurt myself, I would have harmed my children and the baby I was carrying. So, no, I would not harm my children.

The psychiatrist then told me that what I was going through was normal, and they did not feel the need to take me away from my kids, so they did not admit me into the psych ward.

Finally, I was able to go to my Home Sweet Home, and now MCFD was my new normal in life. From surprise visits, programs, therapists, doctors, and medication, trying to find a balance in my life while still dealing with Mike and his choices.

In 2013 my baby girl was born, and Mike was finally off house arrest and moved out. My mental health was improving, and I felt like me again. I continued my road to recovery and self-healing. I paid off the landlord, and it felt amazing not to have that guilt hanging over my head. Mike and I went back and forth to court. It was emotionally draining, but I held it together. The kids and I moved in 2016 to a bigger home.

By this time, Mike had supervised visits as the judge left it up to me to do what was best for the kids. I thought he was starting to do better, so I gave him a little breathing room.

Mike would take the kids swimming or to the park. The more he proved himself, the more breathing room I gave him. Then, my neighbor sent me a message and attached footage of Mike committing a crime with our youngest daughter. I went straight to the police and made a statement. During all this, the police were already investigating him. They came into our home and confiscated Mike's gifts to the kids for Christmas and their birthdays. I was so broken. How could I have allowed him back into their lives only for them to be hurt again?

2017-2018 was when I had my last mental breakdown. I hadn't slept in a week; I had tried everything, even blasting music to drain out the voices in my head. Except those negative voices started to get louder and angry. They told me that it wasn't worth it and that my kids would be better off without me. Even though I saw the signs of my mental decline, it still took a lot out of me to push through and reach out for help.

Finally, the Doctor put me on Risperidone and Prozac to help get me back to my old self. It didn't end there, though; it took time to find the correct dose. Eventually, we made it there, and in good time I was able to come off the Risperidone and one day hope that I will be able to come off the Prozac. But for now, I'm happy. I am so glad to be alive and healthy and have come to terms that it's okay to be on medication. It is also okay if I never come off it. All that truly matters is that I am happy, and my kids have their mama bear back.

Today, I am happy and in a loving and committed relationship for the first time in my life. We have five kids all together who keep me on my toes, and I wouldn't have it any other way.

Now, by all means, this is not where my story ends, but this is where I will leave you with one question or food for thought. Have you ever noticed how every choice you make in life and every event you survive is connected to who you are today?

Over the last few years, I have, and it has made me who I am today. I am more open and sympathetic with those who also fight daily with mental illness. It has made me stronger, more caring, and loving. It has taught me that it is okay not to be okay if you're willing to reach out and ask for help.

As my Doctor has repeatedly stated, there is no shame in putting you and your mental health before anything else. If I can't take care of number one (Me), how can I care for those who need me the most (my kids)?

Lyndsey Scott

11

Unrelentless Courage in the Face of Adversity
DRAWING CLOSE TO GOD THROUGH THE LIFE OF MY SON

"Be strong and courageous."
Joshua 1:9

A mother can be so many things to so many people. Yet, it is earned, not a right.

To those who are not blessed with motherhood, it is hard to explain the joy of it. It is the incredible privilege of creating life in another human being. It is those precious moments you get to watch your children sleep and play. It is the smiles you receive when you walk into your child's room in the morning. It is the I love You freely given to you by your children simply for being their mom. It is the laughter and joy you feel as you watch new experiences through your child's eyes. Motherhood is walking into a messy or stinky room and still having compassion and understanding to love that person. No one tells you how hard motherhood actually is, and not just in the daily task of laundry, cooking, cleaning, but also in those times when life seems to throw you curveballs, and you have no idea where they came from.

Being pregnant is such a special time when a mother should be so happy to welcome a child into this world. I have had the privilege of welcoming two other children into our family. My children are my pride and joy; I love being a mom. My oldest, Zackery, gave me the initial honor of being a mom. His birth was uncomplicated for the most part, except for the last hour or so when his heart rate was rapidly increasing or decreasing because, as we discovered later, he was hanging onto the umbilical cord, swinging like a monkey. My 2nd oldest, Kiara, my only girl, was a water birth completed with the help of a midwife. My 3rd pregnancy, though, was vastly different from the other two pregnancies and labor experiences. The joy that I had inside me, previously, at the thought of welcoming a new addition was not how I was able to feel about this pregnancy. Instead of feeling overjoyed and filled with happiness, anxious for our new arrival, I was now welcoming my third child, scared, fearful, and devastated that the little life inside of me would not be like my other babies.

Oh, I was so heartbroken, devasted, and I blamed myself for causing the damage. What did I do to have caused this? I don't smoke or do drugs and hardly drink. I eat healthily, sleep well, and yet this has happened. All I could think was of a Christmas party I had attended where I had a couple of glasses of wine before I even knew I was pregnant at all. Every time I asked myself why this had happened to my precious child, this thought would come to mind.

I started to go into a nasty cycle of blaming, guilt, shame, and hating myself for not creating the perfect child. My husband was so caring and tried to console me, but it was not what I wanted to hear at that time. I had sunk into a deep hole, and I started to hate myself for what I had done. But, I was not happy and knew I needed to get help. So, I decided to make an appointment with a counselor at the church. She was so helpful and showed me that I needed to place my absolute trust in God; He would carry me through each day, lift me, and encourage me when I could not go on. I needed to trust God to provide the knowledge I would need to understand the doctors and health care staff when I would have so much information given to me. It was the lowest point of my life as a mother, and I was just to stand up and keep going? It would take a miracle.

Even though I was following the checklist of all the right things, somehow, this was not enough. I was told the life inside of me was, in fact, not perfect and would not amount to much, if anything at all. We found out pretty early in the pregnancy that our third child would be born with a cleft lip and palate. Following the discovery that this pregnancy would have imperfections, I was asked to terminate four times as the physicians thought the abnormalities were too grave. I thought these people were here to help me, but instead, they were here to discourage me. I told them to stop asking. I was determined to proceed with this pregnancy and raise this child the best way I knew how.

God had blessed us with this child, and no matter what he looked like at birth, he was our flesh and blood, given as a gift for us to raise, love, and cherish.

I should probably explain to you what cleft lip and palate are. You see, it isn't until the 2nd and 3rd trimesters when the tissues in the face and mouth are supposed to fuse together. When these areas don't fuse together properly, it is called Cleft lip or palate. This means there are openings or splits left in the upper lip, the roof of the mouth (palate), or both. A Cleft lip and palate result when the facial structures develop in an unborn baby and don't close completely. It is thought to be caused by genes, or other factors, such as things the mother would have come in contact with, in her environment, something the mother eats or drinks, or certain medications. Cleft lip and palate are actually common birth defects. A cleft palate can affect one or both sides of the face. It can appear in multiple ways. As a split in the lip extend from the lip through the upper gum and palate into the bottom of the nose or manifest as a split in the roof of the mouth that doesn't affect the appearance of the face. Cleft lip and palate cause many difficulties such as in feedings, swallowing (liquids or foods to come out the nose), nasal speaking voice, or chronic ear infections.

It was confirmed with our 20-week ultrasound that this child would indeed have cleft palate and cleft lip, but the overall severity would not be determined until my child was born. We decided to schedule a 3D Ultrasound to get a little more understanding of what we would be dealing with. The 3D ultrasound was a much different experience than any other ultrasounds I had with my other pregnancies. I could see the cleft lip; it was undeniable. I also saw him moving, praying, sticking out his tongue, and contorting his body. This was our baby boy and was soon going to be part of our lives, regardless of the challenges to come our way.

His name was to be Joshua. As was our family tradition, we chose a Bible verse for him – Joshua 1:9 "Be strong and courageous.: Do not be discouraged. For the Lord, your God will be with you wherever you go...." When we chose this verse, we had no idea the number of challenges we would be facing during all the difficulties that his cleft lip and palate would bring and that this verse would be such a source of comfort for us. We would have to dig deep within ourselves and have true courage to keep going even when we did not have the strength or willpower to go on.

Despite the emotional challenges I was facing every day, my child grew inside me, and I could feel him move around and kick. I even enjoyed placing a stethoscope on my tummy to hear the heartbeat or seeing my stomach move when I was having a bath. The creation and development of a baby are so spiritual, so magnificent. It is incredible how we are designed, knitted together, how our brain, organs, and skin grow and develop and how our higher thinking is created. It is important to deeply appreciate the life that God created from an expression of love.

Our preparation for a new child still carried on, and we were overly excited to add another child to our family. However, this time, we were very apprehensive of what our future would hold and the unknowns we would face. We didn't realize how much our faith would be the driving force through this whole process and the journey we were embarking on.

We were scheduled to arrive at the hospital early in the morning with expectations to experience a typical delivery, with pain and pushing, just like both of my other pregnancies. The delivery was the expected experience; however, as soon as he was born, I could only see him for a moment before he was whisked away to ICU. They were afraid that his breathing might not be sufficient to breathe on his own because of his Cleft lip and palate. I will never get back those precious initial bonding moments that they always stress are so important.

When I was able to go to the ICU, he was in a bassinette, hooked up to many wires and tubes. I went to see him with my husband and two children. I am not sure if the kids truly understood all that was happening to their baby brother. They had never seen anything like that before. It was a bit overwhelming, seeing this little one new to this world, not able to be held tightly by his mom. To make matters worse, I was told I could not breastfeed my own child since he did not have a proper suction due to the cleft lip. I found out that this was not true many years later, and breastfeeding was possible with special equipment.

The nurses were so busy tending to all the babies, and all I wanted was to be able to hold my Son. It broke my heart. I just wanted to hold him tight. I wanted to cuddle with him. I desperately wanted to protect him from all that would be taking place in the very near future, from any pain he would experience. I wanted to shelter him from the looks and turning of heads from people we didn't even know. It was so hard seeing him so very helpless. I was only allowed to have a few moments of holding his hand, but I wasn't going to leave his side. It was not until about 12 hours later that I had had enough. I wanted, needed, to hold my baby. The nurses had more time with my child than I did. I only got to see him in a covered bassinette hooked up to wires and tubes.

I finally got to hold my Son, and it is a moment that I will remember forever. After this initial time of holding Joshua, I was able to stay by his side because I never wanted to leave him alone. I was elated that I could stay with him in a parent room of the ICU for the remaining time he was there. After he got released from the ICU, we were transferred to the maternity ward for another two days. I found this time in the hospital with him to be so special. It was time that I could spend alone with him, just my Son and me. I was mesmerized by his little hands, feet, and of course, the facial alterations. I didn't see an ugly, horrible child. I saw a baby, complete in every way, given to me by my Creator. I was going to try protecting him from ridicule, and teasing, getting hurt emotionally and physically. I wanted to learn all that I could about cleft palate and lip to care for him the best that I could.

In the maternity ward, the room next to ours was another couple who also had a baby born with cleft lip and cleft palate. We were excited to meet another family that would be traveling the same journey that we were. My husband wanted to be encouraging to them and congratulate them on their baby's birth. However, it was a different situation for them, and his congratulations were not met with the same joy that we had. They only discovered their baby's birth defects after delivery and did not have time to plan and prepare for what was coming. They also found their baby was born with Down Syndrome and along with heart complications. The baby had to be flown to BC children's hospital for emergency heart surgery. My husband and I both asked ourselves, why was our baby spared when their baby had so many more difficulties to overcome?

I came to learn that Cleft lip and palate are highly associated with Down syndrome. Not only that, but many genetic conditions can also be associated with cleft lip/palate, such as Pierre Robin Sequence (PRS), Stickler Syndrome, and 22q11 Deletion Syndrome. Joshua was investigated for all of them and more. Throughout our journey, he ended up having so many tests done that at one point, we thought our Son was being used as a test subject for whatever they thought they would like to learn about.

I became fascinated with how my Son looked. I was curious why his facial parts didn't join together in the womb during development. I looked at his lips, how they were separated, at his nose, how it was laying so flat on one side of his face, and how the top part of his mouth was completely severed to the back of his throat. As much as it made me sad to see all of this, I wondered why I was gifted and chosen to take care of a child with these immense health conditions. I was so proud that I was the mom to this little one and that it was one of my proudest moments as a nurse to have the opportunity to walk through this journey. I wasn't aware how much I would rely on my knowledge of the medical field to understand the medical lingo I would hear to comprehend everything we would be going through. We would soon come to realize that others who wanted to "see the new baby" would turn their heads away quickly with disgust after seeing 'the deformity.' I became upset emotionally when I started seeing more 'lookie-loos.

Taking a baby home under normal circumstances can not only be scary but exciting all at the same time. It can be overwhelming with the feedings, changing diapers, sleepless nights, and how much stuff is needed to raise a little one. Now throw in an assortment of health challenges, and it is a whole new ballpark. When it came time for me to show him off at the kids' school, I was proud of his older brother and sister. They made it clear to their classmates that Joshua was their brother, and they better not tease him. They were proud to say they love him and claim him as their brother. I couldn't have been prouder.

While new parents typically only focus on creating a bond with their new baby and welcoming family members over to meet the new addition, we also added in the unexpected driving to the Vancouver Children's Hospital only two weeks after bringing Joshua home. We didn't realize all that would be required, but this would be the start of the crazy and hectic schedule of many appointments, referrals, surgeries, and consultations. With all of the appointments, from the Cleft Lip/Palate team to the Surgical team, to plastics, dental appointments, social work, and public health, it was nonstop for the next five years.

During this time, I felt very stretched thin by trying to do all that I could, managing this new "busyness," taking care of my family and still working at the same time. There were many times that I felt that I was abandoning Zackery and Kiara to attend to Joshua. I often wondered if they thought they had been replaced. Although they never said anything or acted out, I just could sense that it was hard on them. So I had determined that on top of everything else, I would divide up my already stretched-thin life and spend more time with Zackery and Kiara, together and separately.

Our first bundle of appointments was at our Orthodontist. Here we were taught how to tape the split ends of the lips together and massage them down to encourage the lips to come together better after surgery. When Joshua was born, it was like someone had cut his face in half down the nose and to the back of the mouth. We even videotaped this procedure detailing the process. There was tape attached to both sides of the mouth to bring those two separate edges together. Joshua would have to have this done for several months until his surgery. He was such a trouper. I cannot believe how much we did back then. It amazes me at all we had to do just to keep going, picking ourselves up every day and trying not to get overwhelmed but having the courage to do our absolute best to be the best we could be for Joshua and the rest of our kids. Time and time again, we had no energy or willpower left.

From the very beginning of his time in the ICU, meal times had always been a struggle because of not being able to feed breastfeed him. Bottle-feeding with formula was our next option. The bottles were flatter than the normal ones. When Joshua drank, it went in his mouth but came straight out of his nose because of the hole in his ear. The formula would burn as it drained out his nose. Because of all of these complications, Joshua was losing weight faster than we could feed him. Although he had a great appetite, he became so malnourished. I wish I could have known I could have breastfed or at least been supported through pumping. Everything felt hopeless. I was unable to help my baby, and I didn't know what to do.

Finally, we took him to many different specialists, and they labeled him "Failure to Thrive." How dare they? My baby was not failing to thrive. I wouldn't accept that! However, I had to admit that Joshua was quite thin and couldn't gain enough weight to be considered a healthy infant. We had him measured and weighed each week until we could see a gradual increase in his weight. He had a very healthy appetite but just was metabolizing the food too slowly.

Our lives continued to remain hectic with not only running a household, managing work around the many scheduled appointments, taking care of the two other children, and trying to make enough money to feed, clothe, and pay the bills. I ran back to Vancouver from Kamloops every two weeks for appointments either in North Vancouver or at the BC Children's Hospital. It only added to the overwhelm that I had to attend all of the appointments by myself by this time as my husband couldn't keep taking time off from work. I found myself driving through many snowstorms, rainstorms, or anything else that the Coquihalla highway would throw at me. Life got stressful, bills were piling up, and I was only able to work occasionally.

All of this eventually led to us being unable to pay our property taxes. We almost lost our home because money was stretched so thin. I recall times when we did not know how we would get enough food for our children, let alone pay the light bill. It was hard. I did not know how many times we were going to make it to the next payday. There were often more days left in the month than money. Yet, with God by our side, we always made it to the next payday. We did not lose the house, and our bills were paid. We made it through together as a family.

Another unexpected surprise, only months after giving birth to Joshua, was the anticipation of our fourth child. As much as I genuinely thought I was going crazy with all the business of Joshua's appointments, now I had another child joining our family. With all of the extra time commitments necessary for Joshua, I felt we were done expanding our family, so I booked an appointment at my doctor's office to discuss a hysterectomy. The doctor decided to give me a pregnancy test before moving forward, and well, I was pregnant. God knew how much this unexpected blessing would eventually mean to us, but I immediately started worrying that our new addition would have the same birth defects as Joshua. So, when we went to our next visit to Vancouver's Children's Hospital, I had a routine Ultrasound to determine if this new baby would have the same journey as Joshua. We were overjoyed to find out that this one would be spared.

Although life got even more hectic when this baby was born, it soon became realized how much of a blessing it was to have another baby join our family and be a friend to Joshua – due to the age gap between him and the oldest two.

The first surgery for Joshua was scheduled in December for his Cleft Lip. Having many surgeries would be something I would have to get used to, or could I? How could I, as a mom, give my child over to surgeons at such an early age, only four months old? I was heartbroken. I fell apart as soon as they took him away. Oh, wait, because I was a nurse, I couldn't just sit and think about my Son; I was asked to come into the surgical room until they started the anesthetic. Oh my goodness, talk about genuinely falling apart, having to watch your child go from fully functioning and awake to limp and looking lifeless.

As the surgical assistant walked me out, I couldn't hold the tears back any longer. I just could not let go. It was too hard. I wanted to grab him and run as fast as I could. I wanted to be able to take away the pain he was having or would have. I needed to protect him from these surgical procedures, and I wanted to take his place. Why did I have to have a child with issues? Why did I have to be a nurse and know more than the average parent at that time? Why me? It was too hard to handle.

I tried feeling comfort in the arms of my husband as we waited for Joshua's surgery to be over. The Minutes dragged on into what seemed like a whole day. My husband tried to console me, but I just wanted to cry. I wanted to scream. This did not seem fair. There were times in our waiting periods that the stress level reached the boiling point and overflowed. We eventually had to go to separate corners in the Hospital Parking lot until we had time to cool down. The tension finally settled down, and eventually, they called us back, but not to see Joshua as we had expected; it was an emergency. Our baby had almost crashed in the Recovery Room from the anesthetic. We learned later that he had been unable to metabolize the anesthetic and his heart rate and oxygen level plummeted to almost nothing. I felt like I could not take anymore.

Looking at my baby's tiny body, I knew he was given to us for a purpose that went beyond us parenting him. This little life was not here by chance or by mistake. He was here for a purpose. This little life, we would discover, would be our teacher; he would teach us resilience. We needed to look at life differently, with more compassion, purpose, and of course, courage. It was 3 -4 days after the surgery was over, and things were finally calm again that our Little man went home in a straight jacket so that he wouldn't be touching or pulling at his stitches.

Joshua's 2nd surgery was scheduled for April of the following year to correct his Cleft Palate. However, about a week before the surgery, when my husband held Joshua, I noticed that his feet and hands were purple - dark purple. I know that children can get a bit mottled when they are cold, but this was extreme. My husband tried to minimize my fear and say it was nothing, but I could not let it go. I was worried. I could sense that something horrible was happening; I just didn't know what. I had to make our health care team aware. Up to this point, I had viewed my being a nurse as a curse; I knew too much. This time it would be considered a blessing from God.

So, when we arrived at the hospital for the presurgical screening, I talked to the doctor about his purple feet. When they closely examined Joshua, they stopped the exam and canceled the surgery. They knew something was wrong. Immediately, we were admitted to the hospital and had a bucket full of tests done, including extensive bloodwork.

The doctors discovered that Joshua had developed Dilated Cardiomyopathy. I know it sounds like a scary medical word. It means that the big arch in his heart, called the aorta, was enlarged, and the bottom chamber was dilated. The enlargement and dilation were causing blood to divert only to the major organs and not the extremities, like the hands and feet. If left unchecked, Joshua would have had a heart attack or stroke during his next surgery.

Finding out this diagnosis before he underwent surgery saved his life. Wow, talk about intuition and having the courage to speak up. You know that motherly instinct? I had never really believed in it before, but that day changed all that. My husband truly thanked me for speaking up, even when he had thought it was nothing to worry about. We thanked God greatly that day for giving us the signs and allowing us to find out something wasn't right before it was too late.

Now another chapter of our lives had begun; Joshua's surgeries were put on hold. It was now a whole new set of challenges, tests, specialists, and appointments, while Joshua had to be monitored every two weeks again. He had an extensive workup with Cardiology and the Cleft Lip Team. During this time, he was also assigned a Genetics Counsellor to determine where the cleft lip and palate originated. The Counsellor offered many possibilities as to why Joshua's development was altered, from Lewy Detz syndrome to the possibility that his parents were brother and sister, which was sure crazy to think about.

Because of the Dilated Cardiomyopathy, Joshua was started on four different types of medication that eventually helped shrink down his heart to the appropriate size for his age. This would then allow his heart to grow normally as he would develop. It's pretty amazing how incredible God is. Joshua has never required a heart transplant, even with all the challenges. It was only to be monitored and maintained. However, with each future surgery, we would have to undergo an ECG, cardiac assessment and be cleared for takeoff – that is, surgery. It was a whole new level of stress.

Joshua would continue to have many follow-up appointments for his heart – constant assessment of his heart through ECG, echocardiogram, and reevaluations of his medications. Over time, the appointments would be further and further apart, and the medicines would be discontinued one by one. Eventually, just this last year, we were told that he doesn't have to have yearly checkups, and the last one of his medications has been discontinued.

Reaching this milestone was such a joyous occasion. He is finally off the last of his prescriptions that he has been consistently on for the past 11 years. The doctors felt that his heart was growing and developing typically, as it should. So, the doctors had been titrating the medication dose down for the past two years until they felt he could do without it. Praise God! I am so thankful that he has a healthy and vibrant heart.

Joshua's Cleft Palate surgery that had been canceled with the discovery of his Dilated Cardiomyopathy was rescheduled for August, exactly on his 1st birthday. Oh, how I wished, again, that I could snap my fingers to change this for him—what a way to spend his first birthday. Unfortunately, like before, the straight jacket had to be worn. However, this time he did much better in recovery and got to come home quickly.

Well, this was our pattern. We would have a bucket full of appointments and wait for the call to return for another surgery. We always remained open for whatever date for appointments and surgeries that first came available. I got used to booking two full days of appointments when I traveled to Vancouver.

Driving into Vancouver became a new regular occurrence in my routine. I recall one time I was driving in a bad, treacherous snowstorm, only to get to the hospital to have it canceled. I begged them to reschedule while I was at the hospital, but they refused. Another time, I got there again, during a snowstorm, and Joshua was wheezing. I find out he had developed Pneumonia. For this, they had to put him in isolation and, of course, more medications. I tried to reason with them to let him come home; I told them I was a nurse and would take care of him at home, but they wouldn't budge.

Another time we were driving into Vancouver, and I decided to pray for safety. At that exact moment, a moose on the side of the road did a 180 and turned the opposite way. I am convinced that God intervened and kept us from crashing into that moose. Had he come into the road, it would have caused a lot of damage. God has a way of showing up when we need Him most! There was a time when Joshua and I were both quite nervous and scared about the news we would get during that trip. The pastor at the church we attended that Sunday preached on Joshua 1:9 while we were there. Since this is the verse we had chosen for our Joshua before birth, we felt God speaking to us directly; this encouraged us to keep going through all the difficult times.

There were so many times during this journey that I broke down. How much more could I bear? When was this all going to be over? It was like a bad dream with no ending. I was tired of the endless appointments, let alone the surg-eries. I had no energy left for myself, my husband, my other children, and most importantly, at this time, for Joshua. I knew I had a different attachment to Joshua than I felt with my other three children. I did not feel that instant bond with him, and I know that this stems from the initial contact I missed at the hospital after his birth. I had to literally force myself to look for moments that I could bond with him. Oh, do not get me wrong, I love Joshua with my whole heart and soul, but I had to work at it harder than with the other kids.

We constantly prayed for guidance and direction for ourselves to know how to parent well, for safety during his surgeries, and the leadership of the nursing and surgical staff that would be taking care of Joshua. The more we prayed, the more we felt the calming presence of God with us. There was no doubt that God was present. He helped us through all the hard times because we had to keep going, day by day, for us, for our other children, and Joshua, whether we liked it or not.

Joshua started to have ear infections in both ears at some point in our journey and started to have a copious amount of drainage. Antibiotics were ordered in an attempt to clear up the secretions since the doctors were unable to close his eardrums due to the hole that was present at birth. Instead of closing the gap in his ears, he had four surgeries to place tubes inside to drain the fluid.

After the first two surgeries, Joshua started developing Keratoma (cholesteatoma), a hardened growth around the internal structures of the ear like the hammer, anvil, and stirrup. He had this growth in both ears. After attempting five times to remove the growth, it was determined it was not possible, and the internal structures had to be removed, leaving Joshua 90% hearing impaired in the left ear and 70% in the right ear. I was devastated. I was crushed. Never did I ever think or dream that I would be a mother of a hearing-impaired child. What was this going to look like? Will he ever be able to hear my voice? Was I never going to hear my Son say he loves me, laugh, or simply talk? I was heartbroken. Why God? Is this some cruel joke? I got mad at God. How much more was Joshua supposed to endure? How much more would we, as the parents, have to handle?

Another type of appointment was added to our schedule— speech therapy appointments. Joshua went to many appointments for Speech Therapy, and thankfully he now talks well, with only a slight stutter and slurring of certain letters. It was at speech therapy that I learned about sign language. The therapists suggested that we learn and incorporate it in our communication with Joshua. We chose not to out of denial. I didn't want to come to terms with the possibility of him being entirely deaf. Of course, this started a whole new set of challenges. We were now going to be part of a hearing-impaired support group. Yikes!!!!! I just wanted to have normalcy. I wanted this to all go away. I refused to teach him to sign. He was not going to be different than any other child his age. I would not put him in a "special school." Looking back, maybe I should have. Perhaps I should have learned sign language. During these therapy sessions, we were also encouraged to have Joshua fitted for a BAHA hearing device, which was a metal band over the head and a device positioned on his skull, bouncing the sound waves produced. He wore this device for a couple of years until he was able to wear conventional hearing aids. He still has hearing aids, although he sometimes does not wear them.

It came time for him to start his Educational journey at school. He went to a regular school with typical kids since I had refused anything else. He had great teachers that supported his development, challenges, and deficiencies. He remained wearing hearing aids and glasses, and of course, losing a few pairs along the way. It didn't seem to matter to him, in the early grades, that he physically looked different from the other children. We still carried on with his routine checkups and speech and audiology therapy.

His schooling career began great! In his Kindergarten class, there were three other Joshuas, and they were all friends, even some still to this day. The teachers and I co-taught the kids about hearing loss, cleft lip and palate, and what Joshua was experiencing to help the kids understand. The kids loved it, and it helped with them trying to relate and understand Joshua. As Joshua went from grade to grade, he began realizing he was different from the other children. Some kids in later grades were not so kind to him and teased him for looking different. The differences eventually bothered him so much that he started to act out in class and retaliate after just the slightest bit of teasing. I wished so much that I could have taken this away from him.

Fast Forward to the present day, Joshua has had 13 surgeries so far. Each time I have had to hand him over to the OR doctors and nurses, I had to pray for strength and courage to keep going. I still cry. Even though he has been through so many surgeries in his lifetime, I still pace the floors, waiting for the call to hear he is out of surgery. I must trust that all things will work out to the glory of God. I see God's goodness in how He has provided for us, how He has walked alongside us, encouraging us, protecting Joshua and us through each surgery.

We are currently anticipating his 14th surgery this year, which will involve repairing his nose. When Joshua was born, his nose was quite flat and had lots of excess cartilage inside, preventing him from breathing properly. These differences are also the cause of frequent nose bleeds and a bit of snoring while he sleeps. Thankfully the frequency of his nose bleeds has decreased and rarely causes any issues now that he is older. This next surgery will repair his nose and allow him to start breathing through it for the first time.

There have been many blessings and challenges over the years, but Joshua is truly a gift to our family.

"A life without challenge, a life without hardship, a life without purpose, seems pale and pointless. With challenges come perseverance and gumption. With hardship come resilience and resolve. With purpose come strength and understanding." - Terry Fallis

God never sends you into a situation alone. God goes before you. He stands beside you. He walks behind you. Whatever situation you have right now, be confident. God is with you. - Daily Inspiration

Karla Weiss

12

A Letter To Myself
A PATH TO FORGIVENESS

**"Forgive others not because they deserve forgiveness,
but because you need peace."**
Jonathan Huie

I was keeping a secret from everyone for nine years, and it weighed heavily on me. I was scared to say anything.

One day my family and I were camping, and I pulled my mom aside and said, "I have to tell you something, but I promise it wasn't my fault." I was so nervous and scared. I brought my mom into the tent and said, "Please, believe me, what I'm going to tell you is not my fault." She said okay and asked me what it was. I explained that nine years ago, when I was back east, my uncle molested me. I cried uncontrollably and said, "Honest mom, it's not my fault."

She looked at me and said, "Why would you ever think it was your fault." I couldn't answer the question.

Back in the 70s, my mom and dad got divorced. I lived in the west with my mom, and my dad lived back east. My dad moved back to his hometown after the divorce.

When I was 12, my sister and I got to visit my dad for the summer holidays. I was super excited because that is where all my aunts, uncles, and cousins lived, and even my grandparents.

When we arrived, we stayed with my grandparents, and everyone would come to visit us there. We would hang out at the beach and jump off the trestle into the ocean. One of my cousins lived in the same town to hang out with all her friends. My dad took me and my sister camping at a fairground. We were having so much fun. It started out being the best summer ever.

One day my sister and I, she is 3 ½ years younger than me, went to my aunt and uncle's house for a week to hang out with my six cousins. That was so exciting. We hung out with all their friends and rode dirt bikes. One of my cousins had their license, so we would go cruising. There was so much excitement!

One evening we girls pitched a tent so we could sleep out in the yard. It was awesome because, at home, I used to make tents in my backyard to play in. One morning after sleeping in the tent, I had awoken to my uncle kneeling beside me. My uncle had his hands in my clothes, touching me and saying, everything is okay, don't be scared. Well, my God, how can I not be afraid? All the girls were gone, and I assumed they must have woken up before me.

Somehow, I managed to wiggle myself away and ran into the house as everyone was in the kitchen getting ready for breakfast. I never said a word about what happened in the tent. How could I? I was confused and ashamed. I did not know what to do or say. I was only glad I was with everyone else again and felt safe.

I slept in the boy's room on the top bunk the next night, believing I would be safe there. I thought he wouldn't find me for some strange reason, and the boys would be there to protect me. When I woke up in the morning, the boys were already awake and gone. As I became more alert, I saw my uncle standing there alone in the room with me! Once again, he was touching and groping me! I felt so scared, and I was terrified. In shock, I just laid there. I didn't know what to do. I don't remember how, but some-how, I got out of the situation and immediately went to find my cousins again. I stayed quiet, I didn't even know how to verbalize what was happening to me, so I never said a word.

A day or so went by, and my uncle decided to let my cousin and I stay at their cabin alone. We were so excited! My uncle drove us out to the cabin and dropped us off. I had never been there before. It had a small lake, and we had a rowboat. The cabin itself had a kitchen, a living room, one bathroom, and the master bedroom, which was downstairs.

Upstairs were a few other bedrooms. My cousin and I felt like grown-ups as we each chose where we were going to sleep. She picked the master bedroom, and I chose one of the bedrooms upstairs. We carried on with our day, rowing in the rowboat on the lake, making ourselves lunch, kind of like playing house. We were both only 12.

That evening we both went to bed, and in the middle of the night, I awoke to my uncle lying beside me! I knew it was intercourse he wanted this time! He had asked me to take my underwear off. He never asked me to take my panties off before; he would just put his hand down there. I knew what was going to happen.

I desperately was thinking about how I was going to get out of this one. I told him I had to go pee first, and he said, "Okay, hurry back." I ran down the stairs to the bathroom and locked the door.

I was so scared; I didn't know what my next move should be. I started crying and screaming for my mom, over and over again. But then I finally realized she would never hear me because she was thousands of miles away.

The next thing I know, my uncle was knocking on the outside of the bathroom door, asking me to come out, but I was never coming out. I just cried and screamed at the top of my lungs. I remember wondering why my cousin didn't wake up since she was in the next room to the bathroom. Then I realized it was probably happening to her also!

I thought about how I would survive in this bathroom. I thought to myself, and there is a toilet and running water here so that I could survive. My uncle was still coaxing me to come out. I said I was never coming out.

After a long time, I came out as he promised me that he would never touch me again! When I came out of the bathroom, he said he was very sorry and would not touch me again. I kept crying, begging him to promise me, and he kept telling me he promised.

He left the cabin, and I stayed awake all night because I didn't believe him. He didn't come back until the next day to pick up us girls. My cousin never asked me what was going on, and I never said anything to her. I acted like everything was okay. To this day, we have never talked about it.

I stayed with my grandparents for the rest of my visit, keeping what happened to me to myself. I started to pretend that it didn't happen and that I should be, and I became a good actress. I guess I was. I had to be. Who would believe me? I felt like I must have done something wrong. I felt so ashamed. My uncle was considered a big wig in his community. Many people looked up to him; he had his own company, many employees, money, and status. Who was I? Just this little kid from the west, I thought no one would ever believe me.

When I did go home, back to my mom, things were a little different for me. I started to drink at a very young age while I was still back east, and the pattern continued when I went home. I ended up having sex with this older boy, and he was 16. I don't know why I did? But I must have thought that he loved me. That was my first time.

For the longest time, I mistook sex for love. It took me years to figure that one out. When I was 16, I fell hard for this guy who was 19. We dated for a few months, and I got pregnant. I ended up dropping out of school in Grade 11. I did keep my child, who is now 40. It was the best thing that had ever happened to me in my life. I didn't stay with my son's father as he was very abusive.

I was having one bad relationship after the next. Looking back on my life, if anyone were too nice to me, I would break up with them. Now I realize I never thought I was good enough for a good man.

It took me nine years to tell my mom. I had to tell someone because the shame and guilt had become overwhelming, and I was ready to explode. I trusted my mother. Once, I told my mom, I could tell others a bit at a time but cried each time uncontrollably. I had 100% support from my family and friends on the west coast but never told my east coast family.

Years later, I don't remember how many years I heard that my uncle had committed suicide. He'd shot himself in the head, and no one knew why. He didn't leave a suicide letter. All I can think of is that I wasn't the first and probably not the last if he did this to me. Maybe his guilt and shame were too much for him, and it's what did him in? And he couldn't take it anymore. So, he chose the easy way out.

If this has happened or is happening to you, I want you to know it is not your fault. It doesn't even matter what age you are, even if your 40 years old and this is going on. It is never your fault. You are the victim and the perpetrator 100% to blame.

Reach out for help and tell someone you trust. I trusted my mom, and she was there for me. There is someone there for you. A friend, a parent, or a grandparent, a relative, a school counselor, or call a crisis line. Help is all around you.

But no one will know you need help. You must take the first step and tell someone. Please do it. You don't have to live a life of guilt, shame, or no self-respect for yourself. There is freedom in releasing what happened to you.

Kelly

13

Should I Stay or Should I Go?
ONE WOMAN'S STRUGGLE WITH FAMILY, FAILURE, AND FREEDOM

"Take care of your body. It's the only place you life."
Jim Rohn

November 1978, my best friend Joanne and I went to Waikiki. At the airport, I noticed a tall attractive guy with curly hair trying to catch our attention. I thought, "He thinks he is all that and a bag of chips!" He was a nervous wreck but still strutting like a peacock!

On our first day on Waikiki Beach, we found our spot in front of the Royal Hawaiian Hotel. I set out to find surfboards for us to rent. We were having a fun time floating on our surfboards suntanning when suddenly I was thrown off my surfboard going underwater and "Got my hair wet"!!!! And I hate getting my hair wet!!! It was the tall drink of water from the airport who seemed to think it was funny; he tipped me off my surfboard and that it would impress me! Of course, my first words were, "You Asshole!" Joanne and I spent a lot of the rest of the vacation with him and his friends. I was smitten!

John and I dated and had lots of fun together, and I knew I was in love, but he could not get the words out! The best I got was "I love everything about you" after he told me he loved me when he was drunk one night!

Even though we were happy, he seemed to flirt a lot and still wanted to go to clubs with friends and even took a part-time job as a bouncer. I went along with it as I did not want to seem possessive, although I felt very insecure.

I thought everything was fine, but he ended our relationship after 1.5 years. I was losing the love of my life. I was devastated. I went on a trip with my friends to San Diego, but I missed him more than ever, so I called him. I was told he had gone on a trip to Disneyland with another girl. I was so upset and depressed I could not eat or enjoy myself as my heart was broken. I later found out that he had been cheating with other girls. It took me a long time to get over him as he was my first love.

In September 1989, I purchased a new condo and was transferred to the "Burbs." John's parents lived nearby and needed my shower rod cut. It wasn't unusual for me to drop by; the door was always open for coffee. That day John happened to pop by conveniently. He was dating a 22-year-old at the time. "Hey, 19" LOL! That week we ran into each other at a country bar and had some laughs. His girlfriend was out of town, so he came over after the bar. That week he wanted to meet again for a drink. He told me that he was going to break up with his girlfriend and wanted to see me again. I told him no strings or promises, but what the hell. Maybe he had changed? He was my first love?? The men I had been dating were not working out, so maybe give this a shot? Was it meant to be?

Damn, if lightning didn't strike twice after he whispered something in my ear on our date!! Here we go again, only this time I was in control. I thought I had kissed a lot of frogs, but this guy was my first real love. He seemed to have changed and was very attentive, like he had won the lottery. He told me I was always his measuring stick with girls he dated. Whatever that meant. He said all the right things, was very charming, and a gentleman. I found my Soul Mate. A month later, on Christmas Eve, he proposed, and I said YES! I was so happy and thought, what could go wrong? We have it all! We set the date and had an amazing nine months planning the wedding. It was a dream come true! On September 15, 1990, we had a beautiful wedding and an amazing two-week honeymoon at Las Hadas resort in Manzanillo. What a great love story!

I sold my condo, and we built a new house in 1991. When we decided it was time to "Getrdone" and start a family, I was shocked that he was trying to talk me out of it and telling me I could have a Mercedes!!! It was made clear to me that it was not convenient or a turn-on to have to perform on request. I used to cry myself to sleep, wondering what was wrong with me or our relationship. Finally, somehow the immaculate conception happened in

February 1993; I gave birth to our BEAUTIFUL baby girl in November 1993. The best blessing to come into my life! To this day, she is my ROCK!!!

In 1995 we built our new home. We were the perfect little happy family! But again, I was not happy because my so-called macho husband was not attentive, and I didn't know why? I let him know that I was unhappy and did not want to live in a loveless marriage like his parents. We discussed the lack of intimacy, and he agreed to see his doctor. His doctor prescribed some natural-enhancing remedies that seemed to work. But then he would stop taking them, and I would have to ask why? It was now treated like a reward system. He would take them if I were lucky, but he also would complain and say he had a headache. Coming from a broken home of divorce, I did not want to be a failure, and I would make this marriage work; I just had to be patient. I found my Soul Mate. But after a while, I just stopped asking and was becoming resentful. I swept it under the rug and moved on with life.

In 2003 we built our dream home, 5300 square feet, with a swimming pool and a beautiful yard and garden. It was amazing! It was a one-day at a time scenario, never knowing what his mood would be, and we were living like roommates. We fought more than we got along. I still could not think of leaving. I had a 10-year-old daughter and didn't want to put her through having to leave her home. I just kept myself busy with my daughters' school, soccer, tutoring, and my business. I planned on spending the rest of my life with this man and was not going to give up! Maybe he will change! Sweep it under the rug, keep my head down and work.

By 2009, I was at the end of my rope. We were at the Cloverdale Rodeo with friends, and he was mad at me for some stupid reason. I had to borrow money from a friend to buy myself a drink. Everyone knew something was going on as he would not even stand with me. When we got home, I asked him if he wanted a divorce. His reply was, "Well, when the good times start outweighing the bad!" That was an understatement. I went into the bathroom and proceeded to have a mini-meltdown. I didn't know what this sound was coming out of me, but it was very primal, and I couldn't stop crying. It didn't occur to me that my daughter could probably hear me and wonder what was going on. In the morning, I went to check on her, and she was not in her room.

We searched the house and the yard. I called out on the street for her and called her friends. Finally, she appeared from the basement guest room with her cousin, who was staying the night. She had heard me crying, so she went down to her cousins' room as it had scared her. He and I talked, and I asked what was so wrong with his life that he could not be happy. He said he would try to do better. I had decided I am not pretending anymore. He was an asshole; everyone knew it, and I wasn't putting up with it anymore. My friends talked me into trying to get him to go to counseling. I took a chance, and he said he would go one time. At our first appointment, he wanted to make it clear to the counselor that he was the victim and I was the problem, but he was set straight by the counselor. We went a few times, but nothing really came of the counseling. It was a waste of money. I came up with the idea of a couple's trip to an adult resort to try to rekindle our relationship. We had a great time, and I hoped that was the beginning of a new life! It seemed to work!

In 2010, we booked a cruise from Italy and were looking forward to this trip with friends. Pinch me!! Within an hour of getting on the ship while having drinks by the pool, I wanted to get quickly changed in the cabin, and he decided to stay at the pool. The Concierge starts telling me all the rules ETC; therefore, I was a little late getting back to the pool. He ripped a strip off me about how long I took and how hot he was. I tried to explain what happened, but he snatched the room key out of my hand and charged off. WOW! Great way to start off our dream vacation. I knew it was too good to be true—no apology, just silent treatment for two days. When we returned home, it was a very cool atmosphere. He was back to his moody self again, and I was thinking, why am I staying in this relationship of continual sabotage and ups and downs?

In 2011, the year of my daughter's high school graduation, our relationship was at its lowest. It was so sad that my daughter had to witness this behavior from her parents at an exciting time in her life. We were ruining this happy time for her. But I guess she had become used to it. She had been witnessing the behavior since she was small in the back seat of the car, in her car seat, and the home. It broke my heart that our mother-daughter relationship was also affected. I could not go on having my daughter suffer in this toxic environment, and the chances of him changing his behavior were slim. I was struggling and finally decided to get some counseling on my own to help me with my decision.

I needed some guidance to make sure I have done everything I can to save my marriage. The counselor, Ann, suggested that there could be a health problem that I am not aware of. I should advise him that his health is also my business and that I need to talk to his doctor with him! Hells Bells! He won't agree to that in a million years! He agreed! He knew I was serious, and it was his last chance. I went with him and told the doctor my concerns, and I wanted his testosterone checked. I had decided that if he is 100% healthy, I was ending the marriage immediately and filing for divorce. It turned out that his testosterone was at 97%, which could affect mood swings, depression, sex drive, etc.! WHAT? Maybe this had been the problem all along? I told the doctor he needed to get an injection that day.

The next day was a beautiful sunny Saturday, and he woke up like he was Mr. Sunshine!! Very cheerful and bubbly!

He asked if I could hang out with him for the day. We spent the day floating around in the pool talking. He said it was like a cloud had been lifted off of him. He felt like he had been living in a fog for many years. When I look back on it now, I shake my head. You fell for it, UGH! Life was Good! I felt I had a NEW husband, and I told everyone that I never wanted to see the old one again! I had my Soul Mate back.

I felt safe enough in our relationship that I could book another vacation together. In 2012 we took a cruise from Barcelona to Venice. We had a lovely dinner in Venice and headed back to the ship. Several vendors were selling knock-off purses. He told me "No" as he was pulling me along to get in line for the water shuttle to the ship. While in line, one of the vendors had a purse that I liked. He became furious with me and was refusing to give me money to buy the purse. We got on to the shuttle, and he would not sit with me. When we got to the ship, he walked ahead of me. He had my passport and waited, then threw it at me and went ahead of me up to the room. Here we go again! A couple of days of barely speaking to each other, no apology. At some point, things returned to "fucked up" normal. Sweep it under the rug to cope! We took a train to a beautiful Valencia on the beach for four days. We did the Hop on Hop Off bus tour, and while waiting for a bus to come, a vendor had merchandise and some knock-off sunglasses.

I asked John to give me some money (I should have learned after last time to keep my own money on me) he said "No," and he was not joking. This time I was pissed. "Give me my fucking money. It is mine. I can do whatever I want with it"! He throws the money at me, and I buy some sunglasses, etc. We continue with the silent treatment for two more days at the resort – ruined! At the airport, it was the same scenario. He is having a meltdown and does not want me to look in the shops while we wait for the flight to leave. He took a picture of me in the bar, and to this day, when I look at that picture, I can tell that I am thinking, "Why am I still with this man"?

In September 2012, I won a trip for two to Jamaica from ING Bank! I had never won a trip before! He advises me he can't get the time off work and "No" you are not going either! I said, of course I am; it's a free trip! I invited my sister, and that was the beginning of another level of ugly. He was mean, nasty, and vile to me. Everyone tried to reason with him, and he could not get over it. After Christmas, I went back to the counselor. She suggested that he also come in so she can talk to him, and then we both came in together.

Over the next three months, she performed a miracle. She had a way of listening to everything you said and then repeating it back to you, so you hear your own words and then try to make sense of it. Even though buying a purse or going on a trip without him may not have seemed like the end of the world, she needed him to analyze why those things caused the reaction from him that they did and had a catastrophic effect on our marriage. He stated that she had saved his life, and he was forever grateful. We also went to a couples retreat that taught the Gottman theory that was very successful. I was happy that our marriage was finally heading in the right direction and was glad I did not give up and fought for my marriage. No more Sweeping under the rug! He was my Soul Mate!

Over the next three years, we were extremely happy. Our daughter got engaged and was getting married in July 2017, and for our 60th birthday, I booked a bucket list trip to Bora Bora. We were doing well financially, and I suggested that he retire after returning from Bora Bora. Bora Bora, was the trip of a lifetime, almost like going to heaven. The trip was perfect – until we got on the plane to fly home. It was like a switch was flicked!. When we arrived in LAX, he has a meltdown because we can't find the Nexus machines and might have to wait in line. Who was this person? We had to catch a shuttle to the hotel, no apology, go to dinner, no apology. Finally, I said, "Are you going to ruin the rest of this vacation or apologize for your behavior"? Eventually, he apologized, and we enjoyed our final day.

It now seems that the cracks of my "old husband" are re-appearing! What have I done? Why did I let him retire? Is this what it is going to be like? I am screwed!! I am now noticing he is more moody, sarcastic, entitled, bossy. I am not the only person seeing the behavior.

Well, I guess I have made my bed. I will have to lay in it: ups and downs and escalating behavior. I had already planned our beautiful New Years' vacation to Cabo. Just two days in, we are sitting on the patio having a drink before going to dinner, and out of the blue, he says, "If they give us a room on a lower floor tomorrow, I am going to walk out of the hotel" (The next day we were checking into our beautiful condo at Casa Dorada) I said where did that come from? Of course, I am going to make sure we get a good room. He repeats it again. I said, why would you say something negative like that? He stands up, storms off the patio, and slams the patio door shut. WTF was that? He is already presuming we will get a shitty room, and how he will teach them a lesson by walking out? I went into the room, and he was in the shower. He comes out all smiles. I said can I have an apology? Please, that was a little uncalled for. He then proceeds to have a meltdown. Needless to say, we didn't have dinner that night. I was checking flights to go home. Vacation ruined, no apology, the silent treatment for the remainder of the ten-day vacation, including New Year's. He just couldn't do it. I might as well have been by myself.

Back home again, and it is basically you do your thing I do mine, and maybe we will meet in the middle. Unfortunately, I had already rented a house in Palm Springs in April and invited some friends to join us. After the friends went home, I made birthday reservations at our favorite Mexican restaurant. We drove to the restaurant, and he proceeds to have a meltdown over not finding a parking spot to his liking and me not having a big enough purse to hold his wallet. He gets huffy and gets out of the car, and starts walking ahead of me to the restaurant. We sit down in the restaurant, and he won't make eye contact with me. I said to him are you going to apologize or just ignore me all night? He apologized, and we had a decent dinner and had fun chatting with some people.

While driving up to the guard shack, he says to me, "Where is the pass"? I don't know you had it last. He yells at me, "What did you do with it" I reach into the armrest, pull out the Gate pass, and give it to him. He drives up to the guard shack "How are you tonight, dear!!" I said to him OMG, and you just looked at me as if I had done something horrible to you. WTF! We get to the house. I grab my laptop and go into the bedroom. He says, "I guess we aren't having a jacuzzi tonight?" Nope, we aren't!

Two days later, we are meeting friends for dinner, and he miscalculates a traffic circle and takes the wrong lane. Holy hell, he blew up and looked at me like I was the anti-Christ. I had had enough by this time and asked, why do you do this all the time? What is wrong with you? How would you like it if your daughter's boyfriend talked to her like she was a mentally abused woman? I told him he disgusted me. Do you ever get the feeling someone has their finger on your chest pushing you to see how far they can go? That is the way I felt.

My daughter's wedding was fast approaching, and I told him I did not want ANYONE to know we were having problems as we were NOT going to ruin the most important day of our daughter's life with our bullshit. After a month, he came to me and said he wanted me to be happy. I told him that I need some time as I don't know if I can trust him. It almost seemed like he was giving me permission to end our marriage. The wedding was absolutely perfect, and our daughter was very happy, and nobody was the wiser about what was really going on.

Before the Palm Springs incident, I had to book a business trip to Palm Beach, where he accompanied me, but it was not pleasant. We were invited to a friend's birthday in California, and I tried to make the best of it and planned a side trip to San Diego and La Jolla. He was very sullen and drinking far too much. I had already booked the house in Palm Springs in advance, so we went there for ten days, and my daughter, her husband, came down and announced they were expecting!

We had friends visit us when he totally disrespected them after far too many drinks talking about their kids. That was the last time we saw them, even though I keep in touch with them. Another trip ended with friends being upset. No more traveling, I am done!

I would go to bed unhappy and wake up unhappy. Is this my life? Will I die unhappy? There has to be more to life than this? I felt like I had been robbed of the love and affection I deserved. I called Ann again at Christmas, telling her I cannot do it any longer. I couldn't stand to look at him or be in the same room as him. She asked me to get through Christmas and come in and see her. I went to see Ann, and she suggested we both come in. Somehow she talked us into giving it one more try, so we went back to the Couples Retreat weekend. In the end, I knew there was still a problem. I was trying to get answers to what was causing his anger and his struggle with intimacy. Never got it. By this time, I needed a vacation, so we went to Cabo for ten days. He did not drink any alcohol except wine and beer and was on good behavior.

After five days, I mentioned how well we were getting along, and maybe it was time hint hint! Well, it took him another day to act on that, which was shocking. Then on the plane home, he said that the trip could have ended better as he was interested in being intimate that morning but didn't bother to let me know! I felt like I had been punched in the stomach! He was blaming me for the lack of intimacy!

I was resentful. The counseling and the trip didn't work, and we were not getting along. I wanted to be spontaneous for my 62nd birthday and go to Paris with my friend. I found out he was reading my texts on the Ipad, and he confronted me about going to Paris. He immediately took off his wedding ring and told me he was "Done" for the 100th time, even though I had never said that to him. Now there was no way I could take off to Paris as I had no idea what he would do while I was gone to be spiteful. Imagine you are a hard-working, successful woman, and at 62, you are not allowed to go on a girl's trip because of your husband's FOMO!

My best friend Joanne sent me an article.

SHOULD I GET A DIVORCE? 17 SIGNS, YOUR MARRIAGE MIGHT BE OVER! (https://www. womansday.com/relationships/dating-marriage/advice/ g2587/signs-your-marriage-might-be-over/)

I answered YES to every question and emailed it to John. I asked him if he got the email. He said yes, and did I think we should divorce? YES, I said, don't you think we are every one of those questions. I just don't think there is any point in moving on as we have done everything possible, and I am very unhappy and don't see any hope. THAT WAS IT! I said the words! I would rather be alone than stay in a toxic loveless marriage. There was no "I Love you and don't want to lose you," not at that time or anytime after that. It felt as though that is what he had wanted all along, was for me to decide for the both of us. Although sad it had finally come to this, I also felt relieved. I needed to get away, so I packed a bag and visited my family on Vancouver Island for a few days.

We worked with an amazing mediator Patrick Burke and had our Separation Agreement by the end of September 2018. I backdated the separation to April 2017 when we were in Palm Springs. This enabled me to be divorced within six months. As my daughter and her family could move in with us temporarily while waiting for their new home, we decided to wait until January to put the house on the market. I was shocked he actually went on a date while still living together, wearing the sweater I bought him for Christmas! I called up the lawyer and asked how soon he could draw up the divorce papers. He told me how is Tuesday! I walked into John's man cave and asked if he was busy Tuesday as the Divorce papers were ready to sign!

The happiest Friday the 13th was in September 2019 when I moved into my beautiful BRAND new home with my two dogs! I go to bed happy, I wake up happy, and I am excited about life. John refuses to be amicable, although he agreed to it for our daughter's sake in counseling; I have not talked to him since I moved out!

You are probably wondering why I put up with it all these years? I know I did more than the average person to save my marriage. I have NO regrets. It is NEVER too late to be HAPPY! You have 100% of your life ahead of you! Life is too short to be Unhappy, and you deserve the BEST of what life has to offer!!!

I did have an epiphany, that after 9 years of being apart and only dating for just over a month, I agreed to marry a man I really didn't know? I had no idea what he was doing over the last 9 years or what lifestyle he was living. It seemed that the 9 months before our marriage he was on good behaviour and then after the wedding the other shoe dropped!!! They say things happen for a reason and I would not have my beautiful daughter and grandchildren if it all did not unfold the way it did!

Gale Tracey

14

Finding My Voice
HOW SPEAKING UP CHANGED MY LIFE

"I believe every human has a finite number of heartbeats. I don't intend to waste any of mine."
Neil Armstrong

I believe that what we are shown, what we learn as children forms and shapes us. It's only as adults, and when we're willing to look back, we can see how that has happened. The good thing is that we don't have to stay in the form we were shaped. We can still learn and grow and start shaping ourselves the way we want to. Although for some, that process is exceedingly difficult and takes a lot of work.

As for me, my story starts when I was about three years old, I think. It's a memory that feels more like a dream. Or really, more like a nightmare. I remember being in this strange room, and I had never been there before. My sister, who was just a baby, was in a crib behind me. My mother knelt to kiss me and said goodbye, then walked away. I was confused, but this is all I remember. Later in life, I found out that my mom left my dad and left us down the hall in a strange apartment with people we didn't know. My mom had met this lady a day or so before when she knocked on our door selling Avon. She also did childcare, so I guess my mom thought, great, I'll write their dad a note while I slip away, and he can get his two kids from the neighbor.

It turns out that she and my half-sister were only staying down the street from us while she was sorting out her plans. So one day, she came back to the house to get something. I was so excited to see my mom, I called out to her – mom… mom… but she walked right past to get what she wanted and walked out once again. I didn't understand. Could she not hear me? Did I not speak up? I shut down after that. What could I say? I think this is where I learned that my voice didn't matter. I numbed myself from the pain and allowed fear to take over.

As if being left by one parent wasn't enough to cause fear, then came the mistreatment from the parent that stayed and was supposed to protect me. We were on vacation in Birch Bay in the USA. We had a trailer, and it was the one vacation we went on each year. I have fond memories of learning how to fly a kite, digging for clams at the beach, and getting to have Twix for breakfast cereal.

There was room for two on the bottom bed, and one could sleep up the top of the bed. So we took turns, my sister and

I got to sleep on the top bunk. It started one night when it was my turn to sleep on the bottom bunk, with my dad beside me. I woke to him being beside me, taking my hand in is to use on himself. My brain froze. I didn't know what to do. I felt paralyzed. Like I do when having a nightmare, I say to myself, if I keep my eyes closed, they can't see me, just be asleep, just be asleep.

I didn't realize as a kid that if you don't speak up, it tells the other person that it's okay, I won't say anything. But how could I? What was I to say? I didn't have a voice. The abuse then carried on over the next few years and somehow became a source of punishment.

As a typical confused teenager, I started to act out. If I got caught partying or sneaking out at night, I have to spend time in his bed the next night, or he would make his way to mine—one time I had to bake cookies in nothing but an apron. I've ruined a few good tops over the years because I always seem to forget to put on that damn apron. Go figure.

Then one day, my dad met a woman. Apparently, he had a couple of girlfriends here and there, but nothing serious, and certainly no one was ever brought home. But I guess this one was special because they were married two weeks later, and she was moving in with us.

So, he didn't need me anymore. You would think that I was grateful to have this woman come into our lives, and I was, I suppose, for a time. She came with shinny things, including a baby grand piano that looked great in our living room. But then my younger sister, who knew how to speak up in her own special way, started to act out. She didn't like being told what to do by this lady, who in her eyes came in to take her dad away from her. She never really had a mother, so how could she know how to connect with this lady.

So my dad decided in the summertime to send my sister down to live with my mother. Now, we had started to go down for a week in the summer when we were old enough to travel, so we began to get to know our mom. At this point, I was graduating, and my sister only had two years of school left, so I was going to get a job, and we were going to get a place together and move on with our lives. A girlfriend and I decided to take a road trip down to Arizona to see my sister, and then everything was going to work out fine. So I thought. The world for both my sister and I was about to be turned upside down.

My dad tried to get me to talk my sister into staying in Arizona for good, but that wasn't our plan. So then his wife got on the phone with her and told her not to come home that she was – and I quote, "ruining their marriage." Sis got mad, as her MO usually did, yelled at her, "I'll never come home as long as you're there anyway," and hung up. And yes, the wife is no longer in the picture, but my sister is still in Arizona.

Now, back to my world. On top of my sister being taken from me, I find out I'm pregnant. Yup. 19, just graduated and pregnant. Well, shit. At this point, I'll back up the story a bit to give you some perspective.

With this new woman in my dad's life, it was time to go back to church. I grew up going to church and have some fond memories from those days. I am a Christian. Christianity played a role in several areas of my life. But we may need another chapter for all of that. In my current relationship, I felt conflicted. Once again, I didn't know how to speak up or ask for advice.

I had had sex before, and my first experience was unpleasant, and I was hugely reluctant in most cases. But this was different. This man was different, special, and I believed that I loved him. I wanted to be with him, and we had a lot of fun together. I remember thinking about going on the pill. I think I even made a doctor's appointment. But with my Christian upbringing, having sex before marriage was a big taboo. I felt that if I went on the pill, I was saying that it was okay to have sex, and it would not be right. I chickened out and canceled my doctor's appointment. And, well...we now know what happened next. 19 and pregnant! This next part of my life might need a whole book, not just a chapter, so I will endeavor to stay on point.

At this stage, it was time to grow up a little. This was the beginning of me needing to decide things for myself and what to do. I am eternally grateful that God literally put me in my path. They got me in to see a counselor, and I started to face what was before me – and get help. I had the life of another in my hands, and I had to do right by her. Yup, I had a beautiful baby girl, born exactly on her due date, as precious as can be. She was perfect.

Through the counseling I received, I had to look at life in two ways. I had to go through the motions as if I was to keep the baby and all that was involved in that. And if I placed her up for adoption, what that would look like. I struggled with the fact that my mom left me. How could I leave my child? But I did some deep soul searching, and I wanted a better life for my girl. I wanted to protect her and keep her safe. I decided to give her up for adoption to a beautiful couple that would take care of her and hopefully gives her the life skills that I couldn't. It was the hardest thing I ever had to do in my life. I cared more for her than anything in the whole world, even though the pain of doing so was ginormous! (And yes, in my world, that is a word.)

So on to the next stage of life. Several years pass, and it's time for me to find a husband. Everyone else around me was getting hitched. I wanted to get married and have a big house with a picket fence, four kids, maybe a dog, cat, or both. It was a wonderful dream world that I really tried to put in place.

I married a fine young man from a typical broken family where his dad left his mom, and his mom did everything for him, like the dishes and cleaning the basement suite he lived in when she came to visit. He worked at Toy's R Us and was going to school to become a youth pastor. My family had reservations about him, but I didn't know why? Our first Christmas after being married, my Grandparents gave him a gift, a book about "Etiquette." They didn't like the way he chewed with his mouth open and talked with his mouth full of food. This was an excellent start to a healthy marriage.

We were married for seven years, and guess what...we were having trouble getting pregnant due to male infertility. My husband was a person with diabetes and wasn't managing his diabetes correctly, which caused some health issues with the little spermy guys. This put a massive strain on our marriage, as you can imagine. I desperately wanted a child I could keep and felt I could now raise, and he felt like I was blaming him for the situation.

I had tried to speak up. We would fight, and I would tell him, it's not what you're saying, it's "how" you are saying it. I remember feeling like I was being belittled. He would lie to his mom because he didn't want to be hassled, and I started thinking – would he lie to me. I was losing respect for him. One day, while being out with his sister, she said, I don't know how you put up with him. Now he wasn't a bad person. He had flaws like all of us, but what was I to do. I married him. But then I started acting out. I would stay out late with co-workers, not answer my phone when he called. Drinking, partying, I wanted to escape.

My friend and co-worker said that if you aren't happy, why don't you leave him. It wasn't said, but in my mind, I wasn't allowed. Vows were made, promises till death do us part, we had made that commitment, and I hadn't taken it lightly. But it got me thinking, can I? Am I to keep living this way? Although I had love for him, I was no longer in love with him. It had to end. I wasn't talking about divorce right away.

At first, I just wanted to get away, go off to some cabin by myself and try to figure out what I wanted to do. Then the church stepped in—six of them. The pastor and his wife, our best friends, and a couple of elders from the church that had apparently been through what we were going through and they made it work. They came into my living room and sat facing me, preaching scripture and telling me not to do this. I felt like crawling into myself. I felt trapped and afraid. I just kept saying to them. This is my choice. This is my choice.

From that day forward, I realized that we have a choice to make in everything in life. We make good ones, and we make bad ones, but it is ours. We must choose what to say and what to do. I was trying desperately to use my voice, but it felt trapped. I felt trapped.

In the end, I left. I got myself into another unhealthy, abusive relationship for about three years before waking up. Then things started to turn around in the right direction. I remember being alone. No boyfriend, in my sweet little basement suite, and I had nothing to do. I said to myself – what do you want to do. And I literally had no clue. I had a good job, a nice place to live, and no idea where to head next. So, I just tried to live a good life.

This next part of my life starts with a handsome man I knew and worked with when I was 16 or 17. I like telling this story because he had a crush on me back then. I even had kissed him in the parking lot after a work Christmas party one year. But I didn't get together with him because I was getting back together with the guy who turned out to be my daughter's birth father. Whoops. But in all honesty.

We were not in the place we needed to be. I don't think we were ready. At least I know I wasn't. I hadn't yet learned how to have a healthy relationship with someone. Nor how to communicate and talk about feelings etc.

Now we jump ahead 20 years later, and he looks me up on Facebook and asks me out. I remember the first day I saw him standing in my doorway, the first time seeing him after all these years. Damn! I fell hard for this guy! But I still wanted to protect my heart. The only problem now was that he lived in the USA. He lived in Seattle, and I lived in Vancouver, two hours apart from each other. But we made it work. On a Friday right after work, I would drive down and leave his place at 5:00 am to go straight back to work. I wanted to spend every second with him. We continued that for several years. I felt I was happy, although it felt like something was missing.

I decided it was time to buy a home of my own. I was in my mid-30s by now, and I needed roots. This seemed to strengthen my relationship too. He was super helpful, and together we painted, organized, and settled me into a lovely little condo.

A few more years go by. We had our ups and downs. We didn't seem to fight very often, but I know that doesn't mean we didn't royally piss each other off at times. I was trying to figure out what was missing, for me, in our relationship. I remember telling my sister I wished he would say I love you. Yup, it had been about ten years of being together, and he had yet to say I love you. I wanted, no, I needed to hear it. But I was scared. I didn't use my voice early on in the relationship because I was trying to protect my heart from falling in love. I didn't want to say it and get hurt again. But in doing that, I also let him get comfortable and think that it was something he didn't need to tell me.

I was consumed with fear with the thought that if I asked him if he loved me, he would say no, or break up with me. The fear of abandonment was alive and real in my relationship, unbeknownst to him. I didn't want to do anything to cause him to leave me, so I kept quiet. Until I couldn't stay silent any longer, I knew something had to change; we could not keep coasting along. We needed more. I needed more. I was so tired of driving up and down and carrying on like we did yesterday, yesteryear, heck yesterdecade! I didn't want to break up with him, but I didn't know what else to do.

I told him, "We need to talk'. Oh yes, the four words of potential death to a relationship. I remember it clearly, sitting on the patio at Cactus Club, and of course, I just started crying. I had SO much fear in me. I told him that I wanted to take a break and not see each other for a while. Something needs to change. He apologized and said that he had been in a funk. Yes, I think we both were, but there was more to it. I just didn't know how to tell him that. So... We took a break. I was headed off to vacation with my sister, and I said we would talk in a couple of weeks after I get back.

My goal was to take a month off and decide what I wanted to do, what was important. I was on vacation trying to enjoy myself, and it was a perfect time of healing with my big sister. We talked, and she listened. I was trying to see if I wanted to be without him in my life. My kind and caring boyfriend had given me his credit card to use on vacation: Yup, his credit card. I remember using it and saying to my sister, but what if I break up with him!?! And then I would cry. I think in my mind I wanted to try to break up with him, but in my heart, I didn't want to. I just needed more from him.

A couple of weeks after I was back home, he came up to my place. He walked into my house, and I pretty much just ran into his arms and started crying. I knew right then that I wanted him. I wanted all of him and our lives to be one. I had decided it was time to fight for us. I needed to speak up and tell him what I needed so that he could have a chance at giving it to me. I told him he needs to tell me that he loves me. I mean, really. I will try not to generalize about "men." But do they really know what a woman wants? How would he know unless I tell him? I literally let a decade go by, and I never thought to stop and tell the man I love what I needed in return because I was living my life in fear and doubt. Enough was enough. I deserve better, and we deserve better.

I won't say that it's been easy ever since I opened my mouth and spoke up. I have to remind myself that I need to continue to speak up. I allowed this behavior to go on for 12 years. I can't expect him to change overnight. I can't even expect him to change. I just need him to try.

Now he knows what I need, but sometimes I must gently remind him so he doesn't slip back into the habit of complacency. A relationship takes the efforts of two people, but the two people need to understand the importance of having a voice and using it.

There are all kinds of ways to speak up, but not all ways are healthy. A voice used in anger and hurt doesn't work; a voice used in fear just doesn't come out. We need to find the voice of our hearts and use it. Once you learn that, the world opens up for you. Anything is possible. Fear and doubt will try again and again to raise its nasty head but listen to your heart.

Know that you have a voice, and it is essential that you find a way to use it. Use it for the good of your life and the good of others. Don't allow fear to dampen your voice ever again.

Jennifer Robertson

Meet the Authors

Here is to all the strong women out there! - Who stand up for themselves and face the world with a heart of a soldier.

Here is to all the passionate women out there! - Who won't let the world stop them from achieving their dreams and doing the things they love.

Here is to all the independent women out there! - Who have been there for themselves and show that they can.

Here is to all the unbreakable women out there! - Who have been knocked down for countless times, but they find a way to rise and stand up again.

Here is to all the women in this world! - You are beautiful, you are worthy, and no one has the power to dim your light.

Samiha Totanji

———

Kim Mallory

22 Vials: From 60 to ZERO ENERGY AWARENESS

Kim Mallory is a creative entrepreneur. A realtor and founder of The Pink Stiletto Women's Network & Chilliwack Citizens for Change. She is a fierce advocate for creating community and making a difference.

Her life journey has taken her on many paths, and she has inspired women to be brave and have a positive mindset through speaking, teaching, and mentoring.

Whether it's business or life, her advice is rich, and she has been influencing the lives of many women through spirit and confidence building for many years. She shares her business knowledge and personal stories to inspire and empower.

Kim's personality is laid back, and she uses her wit to keep things entertaining. Kim's dose of reality is dished out with kindness, humor, and a genuine and caring nature. Her hope is to spread love and joy and encourage others to be the light.

If you would like to reach out to Kim, here is how you can find her:

Email: kim@kimmallory.com

Real Estate: www.forsaleinchilliwack.com

The Pink Stiletto Network:

www.thepinkstilettonetwork.com

Vannessa Fowler

This Crazy Little Thing Called ADHD: How a late diagnosis changed a nurse entrepreneurs life

Vannessa is a Registered Nurse currently living in Kelowna, BC, with her two young adult children and her gorgeous four-year-old granddaughter and amazing spouse.

Vannessa's biggest accomplishments were finishing school (grade 11 and 12) in only eight months while caring for her baby. As a single mother Vannessa did not let anything stand in the way of her future, she completed nursing school while raising two children. For 17 years, Vannessa worked as an Emergency Room nurse while running her business along the way. In 2014, Vannessa opened one of the few RN Patient Advocacy companies in Canada called Nightingale Patient Care Advocacy Corporation. Vannessa is the CEO of this corporation.

On top of Vannessa's busy career, she finds time to enjoy many hobbies. Jam nights with her spouse and friends, making space vibrate high with their music. She loves to entertain and is often the center point for people to hang and meet each other.

Spending quality time with her family is essential for Vannessa. Gardening has become one of the passions in her life. Vannessa loves to cook, camp, travel, make artistic creations with paint, wood, metal, and flowers.

Vannessa's passion for advocacy and supporting patients is paramount. She knows not everyone has a strong voice. She found in her nursing career, patients needed someone to stand up for them.

To find and reach out to Vannessa you can do so below.

Nightingale Website: www.nightingalepca.ca

Facebook: https://www.facebook.com/nightingalepca

———

AnnMarie Harris

WARRIOR WOMAN ALCHEMY: A Journey from Pain to Peace. A Soulful Evolution Through Love, Wisdom and Bravery

Anne-Marie Harris a Vancouver Island based Yoga Practitioner and Photographer who is passionate about creating community and connecting with others to tell their story through images of love, partnership, self-acceptance, expression, connection, and wild nature.

Anne-Marie lives authentically with a sense of creativity in all she does. She has the passion and courage to express herself and her ideas, even if it feels vulnerable because she believes there is an important quality to living her truth. She is often accompanied by her fluffy companion Oakley, an 8-year-old Keeshond (Wolfspitz) who has a compassionate, calming, and therapeutic disposition as well.

As someone who has experienced significant trauma, violence, and abuse in her life she has taken it with so much grace, strength, love and a warrior attitude. She firmly believes that it is her duty to share her stories of strength, resilience and courage to offer optimism and hope to others, so keep your eyes out for more publications from her in the future.

As she continues to take adventures on the west coast of Canada and experience new things along the way – surfing, ziplining, hiking, camping, mountaineering and road trips across the province just to name a few, she also maintains her spiritual practices to remain centred, grounded and go deeper within. Anne-Marie plans to return to Nepal in the near future to reconnect with the mountains, people, animals and spiritual lessons to tell stories along a photographic journey.

Website: www.littleredwolf.ca

Email: anne-marie@littleredwolf.ca

IG: www.instagram.com/little.red.wolf.photography

Facebook: www.facebook.com/little.red.wolf.photography

———

Samantha Trarback

Resiliency and Resolution: How I fought for a diagnosis and treatment

Samantha Trarback is a loving mother and wife. Growing up on Vancouver Island, she never truly felt at home until she moved to Kelowna, BC, Canada, when she was 17 years old. Samantha has spent her life helping those around her, whether it be her friends and family, or animals who don't have a voice for themselves.

Growing up, Samantha always wanted to use her voice and has used platforms such as being crown Miss BC Interior to do so. In her spare time, you can find Samantha at a remote mountain lake with her husband Adam, daughter Emily, and their two dogs Thor and Bella fishing.

Samantha also enjoys promoting local wineries in the Okanagan Valley.

If you would like to reach out to Samantha, you can do so below.

Email: samanthatrarback@hotmail.com

IG: https://www.instagram.com/kelownawinemom/

Twitter: https://twitter.com/kelownawinemom

Facebook: https://www.facebook.com/kelownawinemom

———

Charlotte Teggin

Mizpah: Until we meet again

Charlotte lives in beautiful Western Canada in the province that claims to be the "Best place on Earth".

She shares her blessed life with her pugs and ever supporting husband who has always been her rock. Horticulture is a strong interest of Charlotte's, and she enjoys gardening as well as other outdoor activities.

Writing this chapter was both emotional and revealing. It was challenging and took her to depths that had not see the light of day for decades.

What resulted though is her strong hope that someone else reads it and finds understanding of their circumstance and solace knowing they are not alone.

———

Thorey Sigthorsdottir

At 35, I Finally Cut My Umbilical Cord: How I gave rebirth to myself through finding my voice

Thorey graduated from the Icelandic Drama School in 1991. Since then, she has been working freelance as an actor, director, teaching voice, acting, and public speaking.

Thorey is an accredited teacher of the Nadine George Voice Work and holds a diploma in teaching from the Icelandic Academy of the Arts. She has an MA in Advanced Theatre Practice from The Royal Central School of Speech and Drama, London, and an MA in Applied Culture and Communication from the University of Iceland.

Along with Thorey's theatre-making, she has been teaching at the Icelandic Film School (where she is the head of acting/voice), at the Icelandic Academy of the Arts, the

University of Iceland, and the University of Reykjavik, along with tailor-made workshops for individuals and companies.

Thorey loves to work on the voice on a deeply human level, embodying it and allowing it to open into all our emotional areas. With all the sounds, without judging it, the voice mirrors everything we have gone through and is a huge part of our identity.

Thorey is now in the middle of her three years of studying shamanic healing method of the Native American Shaman Patricia Whitebuffalo. Thorey applies Whitebuffalo's teachings (meditation and energy work) to her approach in her voice training.

Thorey has helped actors build and train their voices. She has inspired creative introverts to present their projects, guided business people to master their skills in online speaking, and supported academics to find their authentic voice to stand out from the crowd.

Thorey's passion is to help people, especially women, gain the confidence to speak up and be heard, even in the most male dominated working spaces.

If you want to reach out to Thorey, you can contact her here:

Email: thorey@thoreysigthors.com

Website:

https://www.facebook.com/groups/2844249319031220

https://www.facebook.com/thoreysigthors/

You can join her Facebook group, The Voice The Muscle of The Soul

https://www.facebook.com/groups/2844249319031220

Instagram:

https://www.instagram.com/thoreysigthorsdottir/

https://www.instagram.com/thevoicethemuscleofthesoul/

———

Annie Redwolf Murphy

Flame Thrower: My divine spark is stronger than any dark dragon.

This single life suites Annie who as lived alone and traveled for many years. She is interested in clean eating, self-healing, meditation and learning a spiritual path.

Annie splits her time between the Pacific Ocean in Gold Beach, Oregon, where she is the Innkeeper at Idlewild Manor Bed and Breakfast. She also loves spending time at her family's horse ranch in the Northern California Sierra Nevada Foothills.

She is the proud mom of Jessica and Patrick and Nana to four wonderful grandbabies, ages 2, 3, 4 and 5, who are the keepers of her heart.

In 2020 she closed her non-profit Sundance Wildlife, the rescued wild mustangs and wolfdogs due to health issues.

and to make more room in her wanderlust life to travel and explore. The non-profit umbrella included CA Wolf Watch after Annie discovered the Lassen Pack in 2016. Follow Facebook/CA Wolf Watch to learn more about CA wolf packs

Annie's constant companions are her wolfdog Shawnee and Shawn's cat Tiffany, who sits, comes when called and walks on a leash. Annie's thoroughbred mare Nellie, had a beautiful filly on June 10, 2021 called Legacy. Legacy will enhance the families Sport Horse Breeding program.

Annie is so grateful for this life and is blessed beyond measure. There will come a time that she will share her experiences, gifts and life lessons with other women when her biography is published.

———

Cheyenne Williams

Crumble and Rise: Releasing Trauma

Cheyenne lives in Canada in the province of beautiful British Columbia. She has made the Fraser Valley her home for many years.

Cheyenne has overcome depression and anxiety in her life. Even though she had to deal with bullying and sexual assault, she did not allow it to take over her life for her whole life. Although she struggled for several years, she is grateful for not giving up and for choosing herself. It wasn't easy but she is proud of herself for overcoming and moving towards a positive, successful future.

Cheyenne lives with her family, her loving boyfriend, their amazing baby boy and her cuddly dog. She spends as much time as she can outdoors and finds peace within the forests and mountains she hikes and walks. Cheyenne loves her work as a secretary at a school and enjoys the interactions with the students.

Cheyenne also owns her own health and wellness company. She is passionate about feeling good, inside and out. If you would like to reach out to Cheyenne you can reach her below.

Arbonne

http://CheyenneWilliams.arbonne.com

Email: cmay22@icloud.com

———

Laurene Johansson

Never Say Never: My story of surprises

Laurene was born and raised in the farming community of Chilliwack, BC and now resides in the suburbs of the Greater Vancouver area. She lives with her partner of 15 years and loves her life. Laurence has a daughter and a son.

Laurene is the youngest of six children whose mother returned to Canada from her missionary trip from South Africa with her new husband and two older children.

She is an MS warrior and all around nerdy girl. Laurene has a wonderful sense of humor.

She has been working for the past 20 years in the customer service industry.

Laurene loves road trips in Canada, and her goal is to explore every part of this amazing country. She is enjoying this thing called life and is looking forward to the rest of the ride.

———

Lyndsey Scott

Stronger Than Yesterday: My Journey with Mental Illness

Lyndsey has had many mountains to climb to get where she is today. She knows she is not where she expected or planned to be but says she is where she needs to be. No matter what Lyndsey has had to deal with, she says, "I honestly wouldn't change it for anything." Lyndsey believes it has made her the strong woman she is today.

Lyndsey now knows she wears her heart on her sleeve and is thankful to her five children, her spouse, her family and her friends. If someone needs a helping hand, Lyndsey will step up and do what she can, always willing to help others. She knows she is stronger than ever before and continues to grow as an individual, a mama bear, and a spouse.

Lyndsey lives in British Columbia with her family. Her creative flair is shown in her love of art, which has helped her to heal. Lyndsey has turned her hobby into a business.

Lyndsey creates beautiful hand-burn pictures and sayings into wood. If you would like to check out Lyndsey's creations, you can reach out to her here.

Facebook: @WritingWithFireCustomDesigns

Instagram: @WritingWithFire101

Email: Writing.With.Fire.Custom.Design@gmail.com

———

Karla Weiss

Unrelentless Courage in the Face of Adversity: Drawing close to God through the life of my Son

Karla currently lives in St. Albert, Alberta, with her four children and husband of 22 years, as well as her two Miniature Siberian Huskies. She is an Amen Clinic Brain Health Coach, Holistic Health Coach, and an RN. Karla is passionate about teaching menopausal women to rewire their thinking, making the transition through menopause smoother and healthier.

Karla teaches women how to optimize the 4 Circles of Brain health - Biological, Psychological, Social Connections, and Spiritual, so that they may develop brain envy, know what they can do to promote a healthy brain and what to avoid.

She dealt with weight loss struggles herself and experienced how mental illness can be a prison for so many people. She combined her knowledge and expertise and now seeks to empower others to upgrade their health in order to have a better life.

When we as women understand the perplexity and uniqueness of our brain (how to take care of it, making the most of our strengths, overcoming any challenges, and know-how to release its full potential, there will be NO stopping her. This will permeate into every area of her life.

Karla enjoys scrapbooking, gardening, being in the outdoors, and taking long walks with her dogs. She places her faith at the center of all that she does and incorporates it into her everyday life. And most of all, she values her family.

Website:www.yourbraincounts.com

Email:karla@yourbraincounts.com

Instagram:www.instagram.com/radically_transformed

Facebook:www.facebook.com/ryourbraincounts

Linkedin: www.linkedin.com/in/radicallytransformed/

———

Kelly

A Letter To Myself: A path to forgiveness

Kelly moved from the busyness of the big city to a small town in British Columbia. She finds peace and warmth with the people who live there. Most of all, she finds comfort in spending time with her mother, who has been her loving support for her entire life.

Kelly is the mother of a son, an awesome daughter-in-law, and a grandmother of two amazing granddaughters. She lives with her common-law husband for 11 years and her babies Jenny, a poodle, and Daisy, a conour parrot.

When Kelly is not working, she enjoys hanging out with family and friends, watching movies, having a glass of wine, playing games, boating and camping at one of the many lakes surrounding her.

———

Gale Tracey

Should I Stay or Should I Go? One woman's struggle with family, failure and freedom!

Gale was born and raised in South Vancouver. Her parents separated when she was seven years old. Her mother struggled to raise four kids on her own, usually working part-time, fighting for child support. They lived on welfare the majority of the time. She knew at an early age that she would be successful in life and would never have to worry about food in the fridge and a roof over her head. Her father gave her some advice that she may have taken too far! "Don't rely on a man like your mother!" As nasty as that was, she was learning the financial basics of how to succeed. She was given a monthly allowance that taught her to budget. She would go shopping for school clothes with her father, then take the clothes back and pick out 2X the number of clothes that she liked for the same amount of money. She started her 1st job at 15, working at an ice cream parlor as a waitress and a night manager at 15!! In grade 11, she was offered a job in the Jewelry department at Woodward's department store. She saved her money for her 1st airplane trip to Waikiki for a Grade 12 celebration with her friends.

At the age of 26, while pursuing a career in finance, she tried out for the BC Lions Sunshine Girls and got accepted. This event was a highlight of her life, and she did volunteer work with cable television, modeling, and TV commercials. After 25 years, she left the banking industry in 2001 to become a successful independent Mortgage Broker. In 2015 she was introduced to the network marketing industry and found a new passion for helping people to acquire better health and more wealth. She was shocked when she earned a new Mercedes Convertible due to her business's success and her team!! She has also maintained her referral-based mortgage business as she loves helping people purchase their dream home or re-organize their finances!

Gale is now happily divorced, living her BEST Life since September of 2019. She now resides in Sunny South Surrey in British Columbia. Gale enjoys spending time with her daughter and adorable two grandchildren Rilee and Wyatt, working on her new house, making it her own. Her two fur-baby girls live with her Daisey, a 17-year-old Shitzi Poo, and Harley an eight-year old Shitzu/something. Gale is looking forward to her 65th birthday trip to Paris and the prospect of dating some new men in the future!!!!!

Please reach out to Gale if you are considering mortgage planning or interested in learning more about her exciting health & wellness network marketing business.

www.ownyourdream.ca

galetracey@shaw.ca

www.yourhealthtowealth.com

gale.yourhealthtowealth@gmail.com

https://bestmarriages.ca/workshops-training/marriage-counselling-workshops/

https://www.burkeslaw.co/

———

Jennifer Robertson

Finding My Voice: How speaking up changed my life

Jennifer grew up living as a child in Canada and the United States. Jennifer experienced trauma in her life. However, she didn't allow that to keep her down or cause her to dwell on the negative. Jennifer knew she had to rely on herself to make a life for her, and that is precisely what she did.

Jennifer is known for her laugh and great sense of humor; she loves to infuse fun and joy into everything she does. She is a natural go-getter, and for the past 25 years, she has been transforming the doldrums of streamlining business so that the process would be fun and easy for the business owner.

Jennifer is described as a good listener who is caring and loving. She has a vision for her life that others admire as she makes her way in the world. She excels in helping others and has worked with executives as well as financial advisors. Jennifer has done everything from corporate event planning to policy and procedure development and even some cold calling. She knows what needs to be done, and she is on it!

The love of Jennifer's life lives in Seattle, Washington, and she enjoys the travel back and forth. She lives in Surrey, British Columbia, in a sweet condo she bought for herself many years ago. Jennifer believes that living a healthy life, mind, body, and spirit is essential to living her best life. And these days, that is exactly what she does.

Jennifer works virtually with small businesses to help them with the tasks that they may be overwhelmed doing. She wants the business owner to continue to move towards the passion and excitement they had when they saw the vision for their business and not get bogged down. If you would like to connect with Jennifer, here is how you can reach her.

Email: virtualvaluepartner@gmail.com

Facebook: @virtualvaluepartner

Instagram: @virtualvaluepartner

Meet Julie Fairhurst

I grew up in a highly hostile home environment. Alcoholism, emotional abuse, spousal violence, and poverty were rampant in my home as a child. It was a chaotic, stressful, and unstable place to grow up. If you have ever seen the television show Shameless… well, that is precisely what my siblings and I grew up in.

From the time I was a young child, I knew that I did not want to live this way. I do not know where it came from, but I knew it was wrong somewhere inside, and I wanted to do better. But how? How do you do better when you were never taught a different way.

I was pregnant at 14 years of age, married at 17 and divorced at 29, a single mother with three young children, and a grade 8 education, I thought my life was set to failure, following down my parents' path. I was headed in the wrong direction.

But, somewhere deep inside, that young girl showed up and reminded me that I wanted better for my life. It wasn't easy. I had no support from anyone, not a soul. I had to do it all on my own.

Was it an easy road? No, it was far from easy. I was a single mom for 24 years. We lived off government handouts, and I stood in line at food banks to feed my kids. At Christmas, we received Christmas hampers, and I would go to the toy bank to get presents for the kids. The path we were on was not easy to change, especially when it is all that you know.

But I did it. I went back to school and finished my education. I built an outstanding sales career, won the company's top awards, and was the first woman to achieve top salesperson year after year. I was able to buy a home on my own and provide a stable environment to raise my children in.

Some people would say they never looked back, but I do every day. Why? Because I never want to forget the journey that led me to where I am today. And today, my life is entirely different. I didn't just fall into this new life. I worked at it, every day, all the time.

I now help others who are struggling in their lives. They may be living in poverty. They may have a negative view of themselves and an unhealthy mindset. They may be struggling in their career and feel lost. Just like I did.

If you would like to reach out to me for any reason, I would love to connect with you. Here is how you can find me.

Wishing for you to be able to live your best life, the life you came here to live.

You can find me at:

www.rockstarstrategies.com

www.juliefairhurst.com

www.womenlikemestories.com

Follow me on social media:

Facebook: Rock Star Strategies:

www.facebook.com/juliefairhurstcoaching

IG: Inspire by Julie:

www.instagram.com/inspirebyjulie

LinkedIn:

www.linkedin.com/in/rockstarstrategies/

Looking for Julie's books or free resources? Look here:

Free Resources: https://rockstarstrategies.com/resources/

https://rockstarstrategies.com/work-with- me/

Julie's Books on Amazon: https://www.amazon.ca/s?
k=julie+fairhurst&ref=nb_sb_noss

Follow my blog: https://rockstarstrategies.com/blog/

Other Books by Julie Fairhurst

- Women Like Me - A Celebration of Courage and Triumphs
- Women Like Me - Stories of Resilience and Courage
- Your Mindset Matters
- Revealing a New You - The 7 Point Attitude Adjustment That Will Change Your Life
- Dignity - 10 Steps to Build Your Self-Worth
- Self Esteem Confidence Journal
- Build Your Self Esteem - 100 Tips designed to boost your confidence
- Agent Etiquette - 14 Things You Didn't Learn in Real Estate School
- 7 Keys to Success - How to Become a Real Estate Sales Badass
- 30 Days To Real Estate Action
- Net Marketing

Acknowledgments

Thank you to all my co-authors of Women Like Me – A Tribute To The Brave And Wise.

The name of this volume was chosen with you all in mind. Each of you showed that no one needs to let life's circumstances beat them down and keep them down!

You have all lived through adversity, suffering, and for some of you, unspeakable traumas that could destroy anyone's life, for their whole life. Many of you have put yourself aside while caring for others in your lives, at times losing yourself. For many women, this would have been detrimental to their well-being and future.

However, you ladies decided otherwise! You did what many others have not been able to do. You made a decision. You decided, not me. You stood up, found your voice and your worth. You saved yourself. And by doing so, you were able to ensure those you love did not fall into similar situations. You shine and lead by your examples.

Many people may not realize the generational chains they carry from their past and the past of their family members. They may not understand how, although we may not want to be "like them," we will inevitably end up exactly "like them" if we do not work on ourselves. We must make a conscious effort to change our paths.

When we put ourselves first, we heal and show our children and grandchildren how to heal. We lead by example. We show them how to live healthier lives. To know their worth early in life and not have to struggle to find it. There are so many gifts that we give to others because we decided to heal ourselves.

I celebrate each one of you for making your decision to heal. For your wisdom to know, you needed to heal. For your bravery to share your story with the world.

You are a fascinating group of women, and I am privileged to know each of you. Each of you has enriched my life. And for that, I will be eternally grateful.

Your friend, Julie

————

Jennifer Sparks – Amazon Bestselling Author, Speaker, and Self-Publishing Coach

Jen is someone you want in your corner if you're writing a book or learning how to be self-published. Her knowledge is outstanding in the publishing arena. Jen was always there for any questions I had and was a guide for getting Women Like Me published. I am incredibly grateful to have been able to work with Jen and look forward to working with her on more publishing projects.

If you have ever thought about writing a book of your own, be sure to reach out to Jen…

jennysparks@hotmail.ca

www.stokepublishing.com/

www.instagram.com/stokepub/

———

Christine Luciani - More than just a Virtual Assistant

Thank you again, Christine, for all your support and hard work with this book and everything else I do! You are appreciated and loved. It's wonderful to know you are there and on my side. Thank you for being there.

———

Rob Breaks - My partner in life

Once again, you have supported me with love and belief. Believing in me and all my wild ideas, you are always ready to listen and give me the feedback I need. Never once complaining that you "again" had to prepare our dinner as

I was on zoom calls with writers or in the middle of a book launch. You treat everything I do as important, and I love you for that. Thanks for being my rock.

———

To you, the reader

Thank you for your support. It means everything to the authors and, of course, to me.

It is a daunting task to write about your personal life, especially when there is trauma, illness, and inner work that the writers are describing. It is vulnerable to put themselves out there and share their personal lives with the world.

I can honestly tell you, each of the women who wrote their story in Women Like Me do it because they understand that others are in need, and they hope through telling their story, that woman will read their story and decide for themselves to live their best lives. Every writer asks me, "do you think my story will help others." And I tell them YES!

Of course, they write for other personal reasons, but knowing that they can help another by telling their story to heal their life is forefront in their minds as they write.

If you felt a women's story in the book helped you along your path in life, you can go to

www.womenlikemestories.com

and leave a message. I will be sure to pass it along to the author. It would be my pleasure to do that for you.

———

Would you like to be an author in the book series Women Like Me?

Do you have a story that needs to be told? A story that may be holding you back from living your best life? Or possibly, you have overcome and are ready to share with the world, hoping that your story will invoke another to live a better life?

Writing is therapeutic to the soul. Writing about your past events can be beneficial, both emotionally and physically. You can increase your feelings of well-being and even enhance your immune system.

We only get one chance. Our lives are not a dress rehearsal for our next lifetime. We get this one life, and it's here, and it's now.

Reach out to me at www.womelikemestories.com and let me know you are ready to tell your story. The world is waiting for you.